Intuitive Concepts

in Elementary Topology

B. H. ARNOLD

Professor, Department of Mathematics
Oregon State University

PRENTICE-HALL, INC.
Englewood Cliffs, N.J.

INTUITIVE CONCEPTS
IN ELEMENTARY TOPOLOGY

Current printing (last digit):
14   13   12   11   10   9   8   7   6

Library of Congress Catalog Card Number 62–7840

Printed in the United States of America

50212–C

to **BONNIE**

for her appreciation of my teaching

Preface

This book has evolved from successive revisions of notes used to teach a one-quarter course in topology to students with a background in elementary calculus; additional material has been included to make the text suitable for a one-semester course. The course is being taught at Oregon State University at the sophomore-junior level. Topology is presented here from the intuitive, rather than the axiomatic viewpoint. Some concepts are introduced, discussed and used informally, on the basis of the student's experience; formal definitions of these concepts are given only when it appears that the intuitive basis is not sufficiently precise. For example, no definition is given for ordinary three-dimensional space, although this space figures prominently in many of our examples; sets are used informally before the more formal discussion in Chapter 6; the Jordan curve theorem is used several times without reference before the presentation of a special case in Chapter 5.

In this brief course it is impossible to develop all the aspects of topology; rather, the student is introduced to a few selected topics so that he can get some feeling for the types of results and the methods of proof in the discipline. A brief discussion of methods of proof in mathematics, including mathematical induction, is presented in Chapter 0. It may be best to use this material for reference as the course progresses rather than to discuss it before the student has seen the need for these methods of proof. Initially, topology is thought of as "rubber sheet geometry"; Chapters 1, 2 and 4 are concerned with some problems dealing with networks and maps. All of these problems are easily stated and understood, but some of them are still unsolved even after considerable effort by first-rate mathematicians extending over many years. Chapter 3 gives some practice in recognizing topological equivalence of figures, but still entirely from an intuitive viewpoint.

Chapter 5 presents a proof of the Jordan curve theorem for the special case of a polygon. This theorem is of basic importance in the topological study of the plane and the student can appreciate that different axiomatic foundations are possible for this study. Chapter 6 gives an introduction to set theory.

The last two chapters form a major portion of this introductory course. In Chapter 7, transformations are discussed, a topological transformation, or homeomorphism, is defined, and Brouwer's fixed point theorem is proved, contact with the student's previous experience being maintained by frequent reference to familiar functions. The index of a transformation is defined and this concept is used to prove the fundamental theorem of algebra. In Chapter 8 the intuitive concept of three-dimensional space is generalized to give a definition of a metric space; a further generalization yields a definition of a topological space. Many examples are included. The last three sections of Chapter 8 discuss connectedness, compactness and completeness.

Many books and papers have been of assistance in the preparation of this text. Several of the problems and some of the proofs are based upon material from these sources. Fig. 2–3.12 is from Burton W. Jones, *Elementary Concepts of Mathematics* (New York: Macmillan, 1947); Fig. 3–2.5 b is from *Mathematics and the Imagination*, copyright 1940 by Edward Kasner and James Newman, by permission of Simon and Schuster, Inc. They are reproduced here with the kind permission of the copyright holders.

The author is particularly indebted to Professor Harry E. Goheen, Miss Patricia Prenter, and Professor Sheldon T. Rio, each of whom read the manuscript at some stage and offered valuable suggestions. Of course, the author alone is responsible for any remaining errors.

Three special notational symbols are used. Problems whose results are referred to later in the text are marked with "#"; especially difficult problems are marked with an asterisk "*" The symbol "«" is used to indicate the end of a proof.

B. H. ARNOLD

Contents

Statements and Proofs in Mathematics

0–1 Statements

We shall not enter into a philosophical discussion of the meaning of truth and falsity, but shall consider that the meanings of these words are known. We define a *statement* to be any collection of symbols which forms a meaningful assertion and which has the property that this assertion is either definitely true or definitely false, but not both.

Example 1.1 Each of the following three items is a statement:

(a) George Washington was a traitor.

(b) $2 + 2 = 4$.

(c) The moon is made of green cheese.

Example 1.2 No one of the following three items is a statement:

(a) All mimsy were the borogroves.

(b) Stop, thief!

(c) This statement is false.

There are several ways in which statements are combined to produce other statements. These combinations appear very frequently in mathematics, so it is necessary to know about them in order to recognize what information is being conveyed by a particular sentence or paragraph.

Perhaps the simplest operation on statements is negation. If p is any statement, we can form the collection of symbols "not p." This collection of symbols becomes a statement if we agree that "not p" is true in exactly the same circumstances that p is false, and that "not p" is false in exactly the same circumstances that p is true. Since p is given to us as being a statement, it must be either true or false, not both, and the proposed agreement endows "not p" with this same property, so "not p" becomes a statement.

This agreement is summarized in Fig. 1.1, where the letters "T" and "F" have been used to stand for "true" and "false" respectively. The table is called a truth table for "not p" because it describes the circumstances under which the statement "not p" is true. Of course, the table also describes the circumstances under which "not p" is false.

Only one more remark is needed in connection with negation. According to the rules of English grammar, the negation of a statement p may be formed by injecting the word "not" at any one of several places in the inner workings of the statement p. There are other circumlocutions, such as "it is false that," which may be used, but these are easily recognized and lead to no confusion.

The operation of negation is performed with a single statement; Fig. 1.2 describes two operations which can be performed with two statements to yield another statement. If p is a statement and q is a statement, we can form the collection of symbols "p and q" and the collection of symbols "p or q." Each of these becomes a statement if we make the

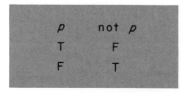

FIGURE 1.1   Truth Table for "not p."

p	q	p and q	p or q
T	T	T	T
T	F	F	T
F	T	F	T
F	F	F	F

FIGURE 1.2 Truth Table for "p and q" and for "p or q."

agreement on truth and falsity set forth in Fig. 1.2. Most of this is familiar, but there is one point at which care must be taken. The word "or" appears in common English usage in two different meanings. Sometimes it means that exactly one of two alternatives occurs and sometimes it means that at least one of two alternatives occurs. (Examples: I'm going to the dance with Mary or Jean. When I teach a class, I always wear a coat or a necktie.) In mathematics, the second of these meanings of "or" has been selected as the standard one; we shall always use "or" in the sense of "at least one of two alternatives," as is indicated in Fig. 1.2.

There are two more operations of particular importance which can be performed with two statements. These operations give the results "if p then q" and "p if and only if q" respectively. They are described in Fig. 1.3. Since many mathematical theorems are expressed in one or the other of these two forms, a knowledge of these forms is required merely to understand the meaning of a theorem before trying to prove it (or to follow someone else's proof).

The statement "if p then q" can be considered to make the following requirement: In every circumstance under which the statement p is true, it is required that the statement q should also be true. This is all that is required; in particular, in a circumstance under which the statement p is false, no requirement at all is made. It is to be emphasized that the

FIGURE 1.3 Truth Table for "if p then q," and for "p if and only if q."

p	q	if p then q	p if and only if q
T	T	T	T
T	F	F	F
F	T	T	F
F	F	T	T

statement "if p then q" does *not* assert that the statement p is true, nor does it assert that there is any procedure by which one may start with p and perform certain manipulations and finally arrive at q. All that is asserted is that every single time the statement p is true it also happens that q is true.

Example 1.3 Each of the following statements is true:
(a) If $2 + 2 = 5$, then $3 + 4 = 7$.
(b) If $2 + 2 = 5$, then $3 + 4 = 6$.
(c) If $2 + 2 = 4$, then $3 + 4 = 7$.

Example 1.4 The following statement is false:
(a) If $2 + 2 = 4$, then $3 + 4 = 6$.

Any statement of the form "if p then q" is called an *implication*. Such statements can be phrased in many different ways in the English language; several of the phrasings which are in common usage are shown in Fig. 1.4. The reader must be prepared to recognize that any one of these phrasings is making the same assertion as the statement "if p then q."

It is recommended that each student become thoroughly familiar with the various forms of one particular statement. He can then use these forms as standards of comparison to determine the meaning of any other statement with the same manner of phrasing as one of his standard forms. For example, consider the various forms of phrasing the statement: "If I have \$1000 then I can afford a date with Yvette."

FIGURE 1.4   Different Phrasings of the Same Implication

(a)   If p then q

(b) p is sufficient for q

(c) q is necessary for p

(d) p implies q

(e) q follows from p

(f) p only if q

(g) q unless not p

(h) q if p

(a) p if and only if q

(b) p iff q

(c) p is necessary and sufficient for q

(d)   If p then q and conversely

(e) q if and only if p

FIGURE 1.5 Different Phrasings
of the Same Equivalence

The remaining statement in Fig. 1.3, "p if and only if q," is an abbreviation of "p if q and p only if q." By reference to the table of equivalent forms in Fig. 1.4, this can be phrased as "if p then q and if q then p." As Fig. 1.3 shows, this statement asserts that p and q have the same truth value, i.e., that both of them are true or both of them are false. Two statements p and q which have the same truth value are called *equivalent*; if p and q are equivalent and it is desired to prove that p is true, it would be equally as acceptable to prove that q is true. Just as with an implication, there are several ways of phrasing an equivalence. Figure 1.5 shows the most common ones.†

By making a truth table for each of the statements "if p then q" and "if not q then not p," it is easy to see that these two statements are equivalent. Thus, the number of phrasings shown in Fig. 1.4 could be doubled by including the forms for the statement "if not q then not p."

In mathematics we often consider expressions, such as $x^2 > -1$, which involve one or more variables. These expressions are not statements, since they cannot be said to be either true or false unless we know something about the values of the variables involved (if x stands for "dog," our example becomes meaningless). With certain appropriate auxiliary conditions regarding the variables such an expression becomes a sentence. These auxiliary conditions are called *quantifiers*; there are two different types in which we shall be interested. From our example, $x^2 > -1$, we can obtain two sentences:

$$\text{For all real values of } x, \; x^2 > -1. \tag{1}$$

and

$$\text{There is a real value of } x \text{ such that } x^2 > -1. \tag{2}$$

---

† The abbreviation "iff" means "if and only if." It is frequently used in order to obtain a more readable sentence than would result from the use of one of the other forms.

Each of these sentences is true. Notice that if we were concerned with complex numbers instead of real ones, the first sentence would be false, but the second one would still be true. Evidently sentence (1) could also be phrased: If x is a real number, then $x^2 > -1$. Sometimes the reader is expected to understand, from context or experience, part of the condition involved in a quantifier. Thus, if the context indicated that real numbers were under consideration, the sentence (1) above could be written simply as

$$\text{For all } x, \; x^2 > -1.$$

Three other forms which have exactly the same meaning are

$$\text{For any } x, \; x^2 > -1.$$
$$\text{For each } x, \; x^2 > -1.$$
$$\text{For every } x, \; x^2 > -1.$$

Similarly, in suitable context, sentence (2) could be written as

$$\text{There is an } x \text{ such that } x^2 > -1.$$

Three other forms with exactly the same meaning are

$$\text{There exists an } x \text{ such that } x^2 > -1.$$
$$\text{For some } x, \; x^2 > -1.$$
$$\text{For at least one } x, \; x^2 > -1.$$

No confusion seems to arise in connection with sentences formed by applying a single quantifier to an expression involving a single variable, but students frequently have difficulty understanding what is meant when two different quantifiers are applied successively to the same expression. There is a convention (explained below) which is of considerable help in interpreting such expressions. For example, consider the following two sentences:

$$\text{For any positive number } x \text{ there is a positive number } y$$
$$\text{such that } x^2 - y^2 > 0.$$

$$\text{There is a positive number } y \text{ such that,}$$
$$\text{for any positive number } x, \; x^2 - y^2 > 0.$$

These two statements are not the same. We make the convention that the order in which the variables are mentioned in the sentence gives the order in which their values are chosen or determined. Thus, in the first sentence above, x is mentioned first and y second. This means that the value for x is chosen first and then, knowing the choice that was made for x, a value for y is chosen. Of course, there is another difference in the two choices: we must try all possible values for x, whereas we need only a single value for y, and this value for y may change when x changes. It is easy to see that the first statement is true. No matter what positive number x is chosen, we may choose y to be $\frac{1}{2}x$; this value of y is a positive number and, with these values,

$$x^2 - y^2 = x^2 - \tfrac{1}{4}x^2 = \tfrac{3}{4}x^2 > 0.$$

Now let us consider the second of the sentences above. In this sentence y is mentioned first and x second; thus y must be chosen first and this choice is known when we are choosing x. Again, a single value of y will suffice, but we must use every possible choice for x. This second statement is false. It is not possible to choose one single value of y so that, keeping y fixed and equal to that value, and using all possible values of x in turn, it will always be true that $x^2 - y^2 > 0$. In fact, suppose someone suggests the positive number y_0 as a value of y; one of the values of x which must be considered is $\frac{1}{2}y_0$ and, with these values,

$$x^2 - y^2 = \tfrac{1}{4}y_0^2 - y_0^2 = -\tfrac{3}{4}y_0^2 < 0.$$

The preceding examples illustrate the procedures used in giving proofs of statements involving quantifiers. Notice that if we are considering a statement of the form, "For all x, . . . ," in order to prove that the statement is true it is necessary to consider each value of x in turn or else to give an argument which is valid for every allowable value of x. To prove the statement is false, it is sufficient to find one single allowable value of x for which the condition represented by the three dots is not satisfied. Such a value for x is called a *counter example* to the statement.

If we are considering a statement of the form, "There is an x such that . . . ," in order to prove that the statement is true it is sufficient to give a single example of an allowable value for x such that the condition represented by the three dots is satisfied. A proof that the statement is false would require the consideration of every allowable value for x.

One further word of caution is required. It sometimes happens that a quantifier is supposed to be understood from the context but is not actually written. For example, the equation

$$1 + 2 + \cdots + n = \frac{n(n + 1)}{2}$$

would probably be taken to mean:

$$\text{For all positive integers } n, \; 1 + 2 + \cdots + n = \frac{n(n+1)}{2}.$$

Further practice on the convention in connection with the order of mention of variables and on proofs of quantified statements is supplied in the problems. It is vitally necessary that the student thoroughly understand this convention; it will be used throughout this text. (Caution: Not all authors conform to this convention.)

PROBLEMS

1. Which of the following are statements? Of the statements, which are true? In some instances it may be necessary to make certain assumptions from experience, or about the context in which a sentence occurs. If this is necessary, make the assumptions, but notice that you are making them.
   (a) $1 + 2 = 3$.
   (b) $\triangle + \square = \bigcirc$.
   (c) I am beautiful.
   (d) How nice!
   (e) I am beautiful or I am ugly.
   (f) I am beautiful and I am ugly.
   (g) If I am beautiful then I am ugly.
   (h) I am beautiful iff I am ugly.
   (i) The 10,000th digit in the decimal expansion of π is a 3.
   (j) The digit 3 occurs an infinite number of times in the decimal expansion of π.
   (k) If that's true, I'm a monkey's uncle.
   (l) If there is life on Mars, then this course is interesting.
   (m) Let there be peace.
   (n) I am over seven feet tall unless I am older than 200 years.
   (o) To be over seven feet tall it is sufficient to be older than 200 years.
   (p) None but 7-footers are over 200 years old.
   (q) All 7-footers are over 200 years old.
   (r) If $2 + 2 = 4$, then either $3 + 2 = 5$ or $3 + 6 = 7$.
   (s) Either $3 + 6 = 7$ or if $2 + 2 = 4$ then $3 + 2 = 5$.
   (t) If $2 + 2 = 4$ then both $3 + 2 = 5$ and $3 + 6 = 7$.
   (u) $3 + 6 = 7$ and if $2 + 2 = 4$ then $3 + 2 = 5$.
   (v) If $3 + 6 = 7$ then both $2 + 2 = 5$ and $3 + 2 = 5$.
   (w) $3 + 2 = 5$ and if $3 + 6 = 7$ then $2 + 2 = 5$.
   (x) If $2 + 2 = 4$ and $3 + 6 = 7$ then $2 + 2 = 5$.
   (y) If $2 + 2 = 4$ or $3 + 6 = 7$ then $2 + 2 = 5$.
   (z) If $2 + 2 = 4$ or $3 + 6 = 7$ then $3 + 2 = 5$ and $2 + 2 = 5$.

2. In each of the following cases tell exactly what is meant by the statement and decide whether the statement is true or false. Use the convention explained in the text with regard to order of mention, and note any additional assumptions you make from experience or context.

(a) For every man there is a perfect wife.

(b) There is a perfect wife for every man.

(c) For every x there is a y such that $x + y = 5$.

(d) There is a y such that, for every x, $x + y = 5$.

(e) For every x there is a y such that $xy = x$.

(f) There is a y such that, for every x, $xy = x$.

(g) For every day there is a day which follows it.

(h) There is a day which follows every day.

(i) For every number x, $(0 < x < 1)$ there is a number y $(1 < y < 2)$ such that $x + y < 2$.

(j) There is a number y $(1 < y < 2)$ such that, for every number x $(0 < x < 1)$, $x + y < 2$.

(k) There is a number y $(1 < y < 2)$ such that, for every number x $(0 < x < 1)$, $x + y \leq 2$.

(l) For every father there is a child such that, if the child is more than 10 years old, then the father is more than 20 years old.

(m) There is a child such that, for every father, if the child is more than 10 years old, then the father is more than 20 years old.

(n) There is a child such that if the child is more than 10 years old, then every father is more than 20 years old.

(o) For every x $(0 < x < 1)$ there is a y $(1 < y < 2)$ such that, if $0 < z < y$ then $x + z < 2$.

(p) There is a y $(1 < y < 2)$ such that, for every x $(0 < x < 1)$, if $0 < z < y$, then $x + z < 2$.

(q) For every real number x_0 and every $\varepsilon > 0$ there is a $\delta > 0$ such that, if $|x - x_0| < \delta$, then $|x^2 - x_0^2| < \varepsilon$.

(r) For every $\varepsilon > 0$ there is a $\delta > 0$ such that, for every real number x_0, if $|x - x_0| < \delta$, then $|x^2 - x_0^2| < \varepsilon$.

(s) For every real number x_0 and every $\varepsilon > 0$ there is a $\delta > 0$ such that, if $|x - x_0| < \delta$, then $|2x - 2x_0| < \varepsilon$.

(t) For every $\varepsilon > 0$ there is a $\delta > 0$ such that, for every real number x_0, if $|x - x_0| < \delta$, then $|2x - 2x_0| < \varepsilon$.

#3. Let p, q, and r be any given statements; prove that each of the statements listed below is equivalent to each of the others. (Hint: Use truth tables to show that if any one of these statements is true, then all are true and if any one is false, then all are false.)

(a) If p then q.

(**b**) If not q then not p.
(**c**) If p and not q then q.
(**d**) If p and not q then not p.
(**e**) If p and not q then r and not r.

0–2 Proofs

A great many of the theorems in mathematics can be phrased in the form of an implication: If p then q. In this section we present several possible procedures for proving such an implication. Only the general methods of attack will be discussed; the student is presumed to be familiar with the validity of individual steps in a proof.

With p and q being given statements, we know, of course, that "if p then q" is a statement. How might we prove that it is a true statement? The third column in the truth table in Fig. 1.3 shows that there is no need to consider any cases in which p is false since, in those cases, "if p then q" is true no matter what statement is used for q. Thus we may confine our attention to the cases in which p is a true statement; that is, we may start with the hypothesis that the statement p is true. But, in these cases, Fig. 1.3 shows that the implication "if p then q" is true in exactly the same circumstances that q is true; that is, we would like to reach the conclusion that q is true. We see, then, that one possible procedure for proving the implication "if p then q" is to start with the statement p as being true by hypothesis and to deduce that q is true; any valid steps may be used in this deduction. A proof which follows this procedure is called a *direct proof* of the implication "if p then q."

Example 2.1 Give a direct proof of the implication: If n is an odd integer, then n^2 is an odd integer.
PROOF. We have, by hypothesis, that n is an odd integer; hence $n - 1$ is an even integer. Thus $\frac{1}{2}(n - 1)$ is an integer, say

$$\tfrac{1}{2}(n - 1) = m.$$

Solving this equation for n gives

$$n = 2m + 1,$$

and squaring both sides of the equation gives

$$n^2 = (2m + 1)^2 = 2(2m^2 + 2m) + 1.$$

But this last form shows that n^2 is an odd integer and the proof is complete◀◀.

We have already noticed that if two statements are equivalent then a proof of either of these statements must be accepted as a proof of the other also. Problem 3 of Section 0-1 lists 5 statements, each one of which is equivalent to the implication "if p then q." Moreover, each of these statements is in the form of an implication, so it is possible that we might be able to give a direct proof for one or another of these implications. A direct proof for any one of the implications (b) to (e) in Problem 3 of Section 0-1 is called an *indirect proof* of the implication "if p then q." Such proofs are also sometimes called *proofs by contradiction,* especially those based on the implications in one of the forms (b), (d), or (e). Various special names are used for particular types of indirect proofs, but we shall not go into these details.

Example 2.2 Give an indirect proof of the implication: If n is an integer whose square is even, then n is even.

PROOF BY CONTRADICTION. Let p be the statement

$$n \text{ is an integer whose square is even}$$

and let q be the statement

$$n \text{ is an even integer.}$$

In this notation, we are asked to give an indirect proof of the implication

$$\text{If } p \text{ then } q.$$

We shall give a direct proof of the implication

$$\text{If not } q \text{ then not } p.$$

This implication, when written out in full, becomes

$$\text{If } n \text{ is not an even integer,}$$
$$\text{then } n \text{ is not an integer whose square is even.}$$

For the proof we have, by hypothesis, that n is not an even integer; we consider two cases.

CASE 1. The object n is not an integer. In this case, evidently n is not one of the integers whose square is even, since n is not an integer at all.

CASE 2. The object n is an odd integer. In this case n^2 is also an odd integer (Example 2.1); so again n is not an integer whose square is even **«**.

Note: Most of the material in the proof of Example 2.2 would usually be left for the reader to supply. The entire proof would usually appear as follows:

PROOF BY CONTRADICTION. Given that n is an odd integer, it follows (Example 2.1) that n^2 is also odd **«**.

The reader should recognize that several steps have been omitted in this shorter version and he should be able to supply these steps on request.

Example 2.3 Prove that $\sqrt{2}$ is irrational.

PROOF BY CONTRADICTION. Suppose $\sqrt{2}$ is rational; then it can be expressed as a fraction in lowest terms, say

$$\frac{n}{m} = \sqrt{2},$$

where n and m are integers which have no common factor except one. Then $n = \sqrt{2}m$ or, if we square both sides of this equation,

$$n^2 = 2m^2.$$

Thus n is an integer whose square is even and, by Example 2.2, n is even. Setting $n = 2r$ and substituting in the above equation, we find $(2r)^2 = 2m^2$, or

$$2r^2 = m^2.$$

But this shows that m is an integer whose square is even; hence m is even, which contradicts the statement that n and m have no common factors except one «.

The discussion of this proof is left as an exercise (Problem 11).

PROBLEMS

Directions for Problems 1 through 10. Prove each of the implications in Problems 1 through 10 and discuss your proof. Is your proof direct or indirect? If indirect, which one of the forms in Problem 3, Section 0-1 is being used? Try to give several different proofs for the same implication. Does one proof seem easier or more natural? Note any assumptions you are making from experience or context.

1. If $x^2 - 3x + 2 = 0$, then $x = 2$ or $x = 1$.

2. If $x = 3$, then $x^2 + 2x - 15 = 0$.

3. If $x^2 + 4x + 1 = 0$, then $x < 5$.

4. If $x > 0$, then $x^2 - 2x + 2 > 0$.

5. If AB and CD are two distinct lines in a plane and each of these lines is perpendicular to a given line in that plane, then AB and CD are parallel.

6. If two sides of a triangle are equal, then the angles opposite these sides are equal.

7. If two sides of a triangle are unequal, then the angles opposite these sides are unequal.

8. If $y = x^2$ and $1 < y < 4$, then $x < 2$.

9. If $x^2 + y^2 + z^2 = 0$, then $x = 0$ and $y = 0$ and $z = 0$.

10. If $x = 2$ and $x^2 + 2x^3y - 3y^4 = 0$, then $y \neq x$.

11. Discuss the proof given in Example 2.3. Is it direct or indirect, etc.? (Hint: First phrase the theorem that is being proved as an implication.)

12. Examine several proofs of mathematical theorems. Are the theorems stated as implications? If not, could they be conveniently stated in that form? Are the proofs direct or indirect? Which of the forms of Problem 3, Section 0-1 are used? (Perhaps some other form will be used; not all possibilities are listed in Problem 3, Section 0-1.)

0–3 Mathematical Induction

The methods of proof discussed in Section 0-2 are available for use in proving any implication. Of course, one method may be more convenient than another and we may very well try all the methods and fail, but each of the methods is a possibility for constructing a proof of a particular implication. In this section we shall describe a method of proof which is applicable only to a very special type of theorem. The method is quite important, because this special type of theorem occurs frequently in mathematics.

We consider a theorem T and an infinite collection of theorems T_1, T_2, T_3, ... such that the theorem T is true if and only if every one of the theorems $T_1, T_2, T_3, \ldots$ is true. That is, T is equivalent to

$$T_1 \text{ and } T_2 \text{ and } T_3 \text{ and } \ldots .$$

The theorems T of this type frequently, but not always, state that some condition involving a variable n is satisfied whenever n is a positive integer.

Example 3.1 The theorem

$$T: \quad \text{If } n \text{ is a positive integer}$$

$$\text{then } 1 + 2 + \cdots + n = \frac{n(n + 1)}{2}$$

can be expressed as

$$T_1: \qquad 1 = \frac{1 \cdot 2}{2}$$

$$\text{and} \quad T_2: \qquad 1 + 2 = \frac{2 \cdot 3}{2}$$

$$\text{and} \quad T_3: 1 + 2 + 3 = \frac{3 \cdot 4}{2}$$

and   .   .   .   .

How might we try to prove such a theorem? The theorem T might be in the form of an implication (Example 3.1), so one of the methods of Section 0-2 might be used. But, because T can be expressed as

$$T_1 \text{ and } T_2 \text{ and } T_3 \text{ and } \ldots ,$$

there is a different method which is available. This method is called *mathematical induction*. We shall first explain the steps which must be performed in giving a proof by mathematical induction; then we shall illustrate by carrying out these steps for the theorem in Example 3.1; and then we shall present some reasons why it is plausible to accept the performance of these steps as a proof of the theorem T. There are two steps in a proof by mathematical induction:

STEP 1. Prove the theorem T_1.

STEP 2. Prove the implication: T_k implies T_{k+1}.

Comment on Step 1. Any applicable method may be used in proving the theorem T_1. It frequently happens that T_1 is a very simple result which can easily be proved or, perhaps, is already known.

Comment on Step 2. There are two points to be noticed in connection with Step 2. First, it is the implication "If T_k then T_{k+1}" which we are required to prove. We are not concerned with whether or not T_k is true; only that every single time T_k is true it follows that T_{k+1} is also true. In proving this implication the methods of Section 0-2 would probably be of use. Second, we must be sure that the proof we give for the implication "If T_k then T_{k+1}" is valid for every positive integer k. That is, we must prove at the same time every one of the following implications:

If T_1 then T_2.

If T_2 then T_3.

If T_3 then T_4.

.   .   .

The necessity for this requirement will be clear when we discuss the plausibility of accepting Steps 1 and 2 as a proof of the theorem T.

Example 3.1 (continued) Prove that if n is any positive integer then

$$1 + 2 + 3 + \cdots + n = \frac{n(n+1)}{2}.$$

PROOF BY MATHEMATICAL INDUCTION. We have seen in Example 3.1 above that this theorem T can be expressed as T_1 and T_2 and T_3 and . . . . All that remains is to carry out Steps 1 and 2.

STEP 1. The theorem T_1 is

$$1 = \frac{1 \cdot 2}{2}$$

and this result is completely trivial.

STEP 2. We must prove the implication "If T_k then T_{k+1}" where T_k is the statement

$$1 + 2 + 3 + \cdots + k = \frac{k(k+1)}{2}$$

and T_{k+1} is the statement

$$1 + 2 + 3 + \cdots + k + (k+1) = \frac{(k+1)(k+2)}{2}.$$

We shall give a direct proof of this implication. Accordingly, we confine our attention to the cases in which T_k is true; i.e., we start with the hypothesis (called the *induction hypothesis*)

$$1 + 2 + 3 + \cdots + k = \frac{k(k+1)}{2}.$$

But then

$$1 + 2 + 3 + \cdots + k + (k+1) = \frac{k(k+1)}{2} + (k+1)$$

$$= \frac{k(k+1) + 2(k+1)}{2} = \frac{(k+1)(k+2)}{2},$$

and the implication is proved. Notice that the proof is valid for every positive integral value of k«.

We come now to the interesting question: Why is it plausible to accept Steps 1 and 2 as a proof of the theorem T? In a rigorous development it is frequently taken as an axiom that Steps 1 and 2 do, indeed, constitute a proof of the theorem T. However, it is important that each student should have an intuitive feeling for what is being accomplished by Steps 1 and 2; we shall, therefore, discuss the plausibility of accepting these steps as a proof instead of merely stating, axiomatically, that we shall do so.

We know that the theorem T is true if and only if every one of the theorems $T_1, T_2, T_3, \ldots$ is true. What information do Steps 1 and 2 give us about these theorems? Let us make a list of the ones which Steps 1 and 2 show to be true. Step 1 shows that T_1 is true, so we may put T_1 on our list. Part of what we proved in Step 2 is

$$\text{If } T_1 \text{ then } T_2;$$

thus, since T_1 is already on our list, T_2 can be added. But part of what we proved in Step 2 is

$$\text{If } T_2 \text{ then } T_3;$$

thus, since T_2 is already on our list, T_3 can be added. Again, part of what we proved in Step 2 is

$$\text{If } T_3 \text{ then } T_4;$$

thus T_4 can be added to our list. $\ldots$, etc., $\ldots$. The list of theorems which Steps 1 and 2 show to be true, therefore, contains all of the theorems $T_1, T_2, T_3, \ldots$; and this means that the theorem T is true.

We can now see why it is important that the proof we give in Step 2 should be valid for every positive integral value of k. In order to be sure that our list contains *all* of the theorems $T_1, T_2, T_3, \ldots$ we must use, successively, every one of the implications

$$\text{If } T_1 \text{ then } T_2.$$
$$\text{If } T_2 \text{ then } T_3.$$
$$\text{If } T_3 \text{ then } T_4.$$

$$\cdot \quad \cdot \quad \cdot$$

Thus we must be sure that the proof in Step 2 really does prove every one of these implications; i.e., it must be valid for all positive integral values of k.

Example 3.2 If n is any integer larger than 3, then $2^n < n!$

PROOF BY MATHEMATICAL INDUCTION. We are to consider the values $n = 4$, 5, 6, $\ldots$; so the theorem T which we have to prove easily breaks up into the following infinite collection of theorems:

$$T_1: \qquad 2^4 < 4!$$

$$T_2: \qquad 2^5 < 5!$$

$$T_3: \qquad 2^6 < 6!$$

. . .

$$T_k: \qquad 2^{(k+3)} < (k+3)!$$

$$T_{k+1}: \quad 2^{(k+4)} < (k+4)!$$

. . .

Thus our theorem is one to which mathematical induction is applicable. (These preliminaries are usually not given in a proof by mathematical induction, but the student should convince himself in each case that the theorem is one to which mathematical induction applies.)

STEP 1. We must prove that $2^4 < 4!$ But this is just the statement $16 < 24$, which is well-known to be true.

STEP 2. We must prove the implication

$$\text{If } 2^{k+3} < (k+3)! \text{ then } 2^{k+4} < (k+4)!$$

We shall give a direct proof; we have, therefore, by the induction hypothesis,

$$2^{k+3} < (k+3)!$$

But, for any positive integer k, $2 < k + 4$. Multiplying corresponding members of these inequalities, we obtain

$$2 \cdot 2^{k+3} = 2^{k+4} < (k+3)!\,(k+4) = (k+4)!$$

which is the required result «.

There is a somewhat different procedure which is also acceptable as a proof of a theorem of the type we have been discussing. This procedure also goes by the name of mathematical induction. We shall call it mathematical induction, Type 2, to distinguish it from the former version, Type 1; we shall explain the steps which must be performed in this procedure and shall illustrate them by carrying out the steps in Example 3.3 below. It is left as an exercise (Problem 12) to discuss the plausibility of accepting this procedure as a proof. We shall need both of these types of mathematical induction in our discussion of maps.

Let $T_1, T_2, T_3, \ldots$ be an infinite collection of theorems and let T be a theorem which is true iff every one of the theorems $T_1, T_2, T_3, \ldots$ is true. The following two steps are acceptable as a proof of the theorem T.

STEP 1. Prove the theorem T_1.

STEP 2. Prove the implication

If T_1 and T_2 and T_3 and ... and T_{k-1} then T_k.

Comment on Step 1. This is the same as Step 1 in Type 1 induction; it can be shown that Step 1 is not actually necessary in mathematical induction, Type 2, but we shall not go into the matter here. (Caution: Step 1 *is* necessary in Type 1 induction.)

Comment on Step 2. Again, Step 2 is to prove a certain implication. We are not concerned with whether or not the separate theorems T_1, T_2, etc. are true; all we need to do in Step 2 is to prove that the implication stated is true. As with Type 1 induction, we must be careful that the proof we give for the implication in Step 2 is valid for any positive integral value of k. In comparing this Step 2 with the Step 2 in Type 1 induction, we see that, in Type 1, we prove each of the theorems T_1, T_2, T_3, ... (except the first) from the hypothesis that the particular theorem just before it is true. In Type 2, we prove each theorem from the hypothesis that every one of the theorems before it is true.

Example **3.3** If n is an integer larger than 1, then either n is a prime or n can be expressed as a product of primes.
PROOF BY MATHEMATICAL INDUCTION. We shall use Type 2 induction; the student should convince himself that this theorem is one to which mathematical induction is applicable.

STEP 1. We consider the value $n = 2$; since 2 is a prime, the theorem is true in this case.

STEP 2. We consider an arbitrary integer $n_0 > 1$. By the induction hypothesis, each integer m such that $1 < m < n_0$ is either a prime or a product of primes; we must prove that n_0 is a prime or a product of primes. The proof is made in two cases.

CASE 1. The number n_0 is a prime. In this case the implication is evidently true.

CASE 2. The number n_0 is not a prime. In this case n_0 has a positive integral factor p such that $1 < p < n_0$. Thus $n_0 = p \cdot q$ where each one of p and q is an integer larger than 1 and less than n_0. By the induction hypothesis, each of p and q is either a prime or a product of primes. Thus n_0 is a product of primes **«**.

PROBLEMS

Directions for Problems 1 through 11. Use mathematical induction to prove each of the results in Problems 1 through 11. Which type of induction seems most natural in each case? Try to prove each result without using induction.

1. If n is any positive integer then

$$\frac{1}{1 \cdot 2} + \frac{1}{2 \cdot 3} + \cdots + \frac{1}{n(n+1)} = \frac{n}{n+1}.$$

2. If n is any non-negative integer then $2^n > n$.

3. In any convex polygon with n sides the sum of the angles is $(n-2)180$ deg. (Hint: By a theorem of plane geometry the sum of the angles of a triangle is 180 deg.)

4. Let n be a positive integer; in any set of n real numbers there is a largest one.

5. For any positive integer n

$$1 \cdot 3 + 2 \cdot 4 + 3 \cdot 5 + \cdots + n(n+2) = \frac{n}{6}(n+1)(2n+7).$$

6. If n is an integer larger than 1, then the maximum number of points of intersection of n distinct lines in a plane is $\frac{1}{2}n(n-1)$.

7. If n is any positive integer then

$$1^3 + 2^3 + 3^3 + \cdots + n^3 = \frac{n^2(n+1)^2}{4}.$$

8. If n is an integer greater than 1, then the number of prime factors of n is less than $2 \log_e n$.

9. If n is a non-negative integer, then $n^2 < 4^n$. [Hint: First prove (without using induction) that, for any positive integer n, $2n + 1 \leq 3n^2$.]

10. If n is any positive integer, then $a - b$ is a factor of $a^n - b^n$. [Hint: $a^n - b^n = (a^n - ba^{n-1}) + (ba^{n-1} - b^n)$.]

11. If n and m are any positive integers, prove that there is a non-negative integer q and an integer r such that $0 \leq r < m$ and $n = mq + r$. Prove also that the integers q and r are uniquely determined by n and m.

12. Discuss the plausibility of accepting the procedure of mathematical induction, Type 2 as a proof the theorem T.

13. Discuss the following "proof" of the (false) theorem: If n is any positive integer and S is a set containing exactly n real numbers, then all the numbers in S are equal.

PROOF BY INDUCTION. STEP 1. If $n = 1$ the result is evident.

STEP 2. By the induction hypothesis the result is true when $n = k$; we must prove that it is correct when $n = k + 1$. Let S be any set containing exactly $k + 1$ real numbers and denote these real numbers by $a_1, a_2, a_3, \ldots,$ a_k, a_{k+1}. If we omit a_{k+1} from this list, we obtain exactly k numbers $a_1, a_2, \ldots,$ a_k; by the induction hypothesis these numbers are all equal.

$$a_1 = a_2 = \cdots = a_k.$$

If we omit a_1 from the list of numbers in S we again obtain exactly k numbers $a_2, a_3, \cdots, a_k, a_{k+1}$; by the induction hypothesis these numbers are all equal.

$$a_2 = a_3 = \cdots = a_k = a_{k+1}.$$

It follows easily that all $k + 1$ numbers in S are equal **.

What is Topology?

1–1 A Glance at Euclidean Geometry

A formal definition of topology is given in Section 7-3; an intuitive feeling for the subject will suffice for the present. This intuitive feeling can be developed by noticing the similarities, and the differences, between topology and ordinary (Euclidean) high school geometry.

Euclidean geometry is the study of certain properties of figures in a plane or in space. Not all properties of a figure are of interest — only the "geometric" properties. But how can we tell whether or not a certain property is a geometric one? For example, we might notice the follow-

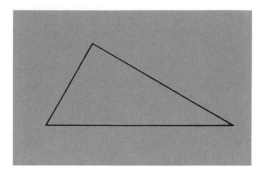

FIGURE 1.1

ing properties of the triangle shown in Fig. 1.1:

(1) The length of the longest side is about 2 inches.

(2) The triangle is drawn in black ink.

(3) One angle is about 90 deg.

(4) The triangle is drawn near the left-hand edge of the page.

(5) The angle which is about 90 deg is higher on the page than either of the other angles.

Which of these are geometric properties?

The answer to this question can be based on the concept of congruent figures; two figures are called congruent iff one of them can be placed upon the other so that the two figures exactly coincide. A geometric property of a figure is a property which is also enjoyed by every congruent figure. That is, all congruent figures are the same to a geometer and, in studying a certain figure, he is interested only in properties which are common to all the figures congruent to that one. It is now easy to see that properties 1 and 3 above are geometric properties of the triangle in Fig. 1.1 since these properties will also be possessed by any triangle congruent to the given one. Properties 2, 4, and 5 are not geometric properties, since a triangle congruent to the given triangle may fail to have these properties. The property of having four corners is a geometric property, as is the property of being a pentagon; other examples appear in the problems.

1–2 What is Topology?

It is surprising that a fairly satisfactory description of topology can be obtained by changing "geometry" to "topology," "geometric" to "topological," etc. in Section 1-1 above, and by changing the interpretation of one phrase. The reason that this material describes both geometry and topology is that the only difference between the two has been wrapped up and hidden in the phrase "can be placed upon," which appears in the definition of "congruent." Let us examine this phrase more closely. How do we "place" a figure? How can we move it? What are we allowed to do to it on the way? In geometry, the movements we are allowed are the rigid motions (translations, rotations, reflections), in which the distance between any two points of the figure is not changed. Thus, the geometric properties are those which are invariant under the rigid motions — any rigid motion of a figure makes no change at all in the geometric properties of the figure.

In topology, the movements we are allowed might be called the elastic motions. We imagine that our figures are made of perfectly elastic rubber and, in moving a figure, we can stretch, twist, pull, and bend it at pleasure. We are even allowed to cut such a rubber figure and tie it in a knot, provided that we later sew up the cut exactly as it was before; that is, so that points which were close together before we cut the figure are close together after the cut is sewed up. However, we must be careful that distinct points in a figure remain distinct; we are not allowed to force two

FIGURE 2.1

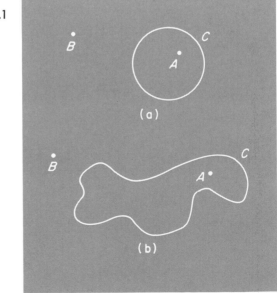

different points to coalesce into just one point. Two figures are *topologically equivalent* iff one figure can be made to coincide with the other by an elastic motion. The topological properties of a figure are those which are also enjoyed by all topologically equivalent figures. That is, all topologically equivalent figures are the same to a topologist and, in studying a certain figure, he is interested only in properties which are common to all the figures which are topologically equivalent to that one. Thus the topological properties of a figure are those which are invariant under the elastic motions — any elastic motion of a figure makes no change at all in the topological properties of the figure. Of course, topology is the study of topological properties of figures.

Certainly, any topological property of a figure is also a geometric property of that figure, but many geometric properties are not topological properties. The topological properties of a figure can be only the most basic and fundamental of its geometric properties. In fact, it might appear at first glance that no property is a topological one — that any property of a figure could be changed by some elastic motion! Fortunately, this is not the case. For instance, a circle C (Fig. 2.1a) divides the points of a plane into 3 sets — the points inside the circle, the points on the circle, and the points outside the circle. This property of a circle in a plane is a topological property, for, if we imagine that the circle and the two points A and B are marked on a perfectly elastic sheet of rubber, and that the figure is subjected to an elastic motion, the result might be a

FIGURE 2.2

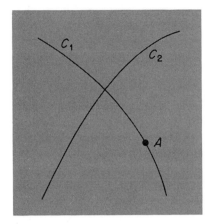

FIGURE 2.3

curve C and two points A and B, such as are shown in Fig. 2.1b. The points A and B are, respectively, inside and outside the circle (Fig. 2.1a) and, after the elastic motion of this sheet of rubber, the points A and B are still, respectively, inside and outside the curve C (Fig. 2.1b). Thus, the property "A is inside the curve C" is a topological property of the original figure. The property "A is closer to C than B is" is not a topological property, since, by an elastic motion, we can arrange that B is very close to C while A is far from C.

As another illustration, the circle and the knotted curve shown in Fig. 2.2 are topologically equivalent. If we imagine a rubber band in the

FIGURE 2.4

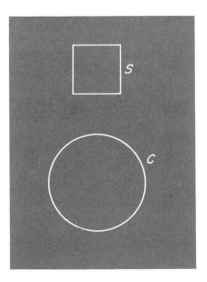

shape of a circle, it is not possible to make it into a knot just by stretching it, but it is quite easy to obtain the knotted curve by first cutting the rubber band, then tying the knot, and finally joining the two ends as they were before. Since these manipulations are allowed under what we have called an elastic motion, the two curves are topologically equivalent. Other examples are given in the problems.

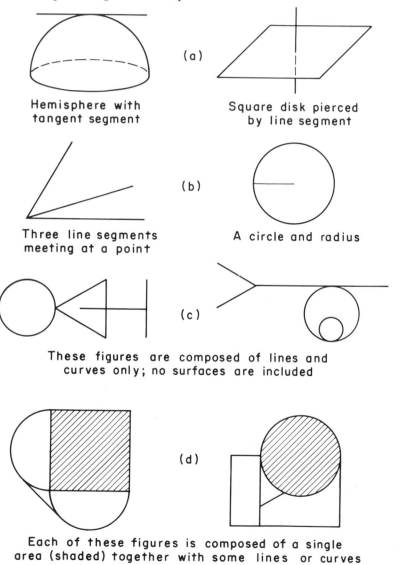

(a)

Hemisphere with
tangent segment

Square disk pierced
by line segment

(b)

Three line segments
meeting at a point

A circle and radius

(c)

These figures are composed of lines and
curves only; no surfaces are included

(d)

Each of these figures is composed of a single
area (shaded) together with some lines or curves

FIGURE 2.5

PROBLEMS

1. (a) For each of the properties 2, 4, and 5 noted in connection with Fig. 1.1, find a triangle congruent to the one shown, which does not have the property.
   (b) Find an elastic motion of the plane of Fig. 2.1a which will arrange that the point B is closer to the curve C than A is.

Directions for Problems 2 and 3. Several properties are noted for each of Figs. 2.3 and 2.4. Which are geometric properties? Which are topological properties?

2. The following properties refer to Fig. 2.3.
   (a) The curves C_1 and C_2 intersect.
   (b) The curves C_1 and C_2 are perpendicular.
   (c) The curves C_1 and C_2 are not tangent.
   (d) The point A is on the curve C_1.
   (e) The point A is not on the curve C_2.
   (f) The point A is below the curve C_2.
   (g) The curve C_2 is concave toward the point A.

3. The following properties refer to Fig. 2.4.
   (a) The figure consists of a square and a circle drawn in a plane.
   (b) The figure consists of two curves drawn in a plane; one of them has four corners and the other one is smooth.
   (c) The area enclosed by the curve S is smaller than the area enclosed by the curve C.
   (d) The area enclosed by the upper curve is smaller than the area enclosed by the lower curve.
   (e) The curves S and C do not intersect.
   (f) No point is enclosed by both the curves S and C.

#4. Four pairs of figures are shown in Fig. 2.5. Which of these pairs of figures are topologically equivalent?

Networks and Maps

2–1 Traversability of Networks

The city of Königsberg (now called Kaliningrad) in Western Russia stands where the New Pregel and Old Pregel Rivers join to form the Pregel River; there is an island formed at the point of confluence. In the eighteenth century there were seven bridges, as shown in Fig. 1.1 (two more bridges have since been built). It was asked whether or not it would be possible to make a walking tour of Königsberg and cross each of the bridges exactly once. This question, along with many related problems, was settled

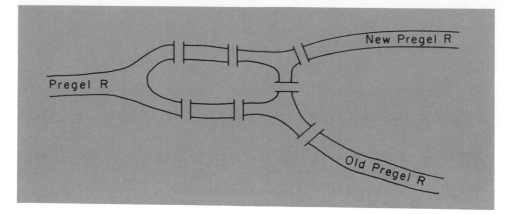

FIGURE 1.1

by the Swiss mathematician Leonhard Euler (1707-1783) in 1736, as indicated below.

First, notice that the actual shape of the river bank, the position of the island, etc. are of no importance; Fig. 1.1 could be replaced by the simpler Fig. 1.2, which shows how the various sections of the city are interconnected by bridges. The point A in Fig. 1.2 represents the entire section of the city lying to the north of the river; similarly, D represents the section south of the river, B represents the area between the New and the Old Pregel, and C represents the island section. The bridges connecting various sections of the city are represented by line segments or pieces of curves. A line segment, or a curve which can be obtained by an elastic motion of a line segment, will be called an *arc*. We shall even allow the two end points of an arc to be brought together (forming a curve like a circle) and shall still call the figure an arc, but an arc cannot have any intersections with itself except at the two end points. (Caution: We are departing from the standard terminology here. The end points of an arc are usually required to be two different points, but we will find it convenient to allow them to be the same point.) The study of the Königsberg bridges has led us to a figure composed of seven arcs and four points.

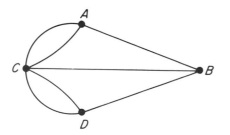

FIGURE 1.2

Before we continue with Euler's solution, it will be convenient to have some general terminology which will also be of interest in other connections.

A *network* is a figure (in a plane or in space) consisting of a finite, non-zero, number of arcs, no two of which intersect except possibly at their end points. The end points of these arcs are called *vertices* (singular: *vertex*) of the network. Figure 1.2 shows an example of a network with seven arcs and four vertices. Other examples of networks are shown in Fig. 1.3. The points which are vertices are depicted by enlarged dots

FIGURE 1.3   Examples of Networks

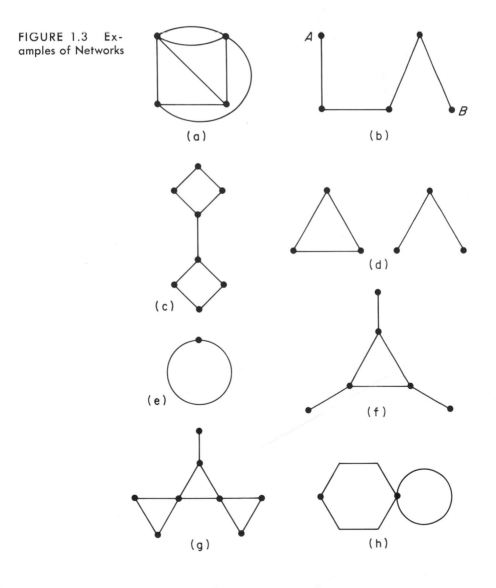

(a)

(b)

(c)

(d)

(e)

(f)

(g)

(h)

in this figure. We shall not always use this convention and, when it is not used, it is sometimes necessary to decide somewhat arbitrarily which points are vertices. For example, in Fig. 1.3b the points A and B must be vertices; any of the other points could have been chosen as vertices.

The *order* of a vertex in a network is the number of arc ends at that vertex. A vertex is *odd* or *even* iff its order is odd or even, respectively. In Fig. 1.2, each of the vertices A, B, and D is of order 3; vertex C is of order 5; each of the four vertices is odd. In Fig. 1.3e, the only vertex is even, and of order 2, since there are two arc ends at the vertex. In fact, these two arc ends are the two opposite ends of the same arc.

The total number of arcs in a network could be any positive integer; similarly, the total number of vertices is unrestricted. On the other hand, each arc has two ends, so the total number of arc ends is twice the number of arcs, and hence is even. But the total number of arc ends in a network is the sum of the orders of all the vertices of the network; thus, in any network, the sum of the orders of all the vertices of the network must be a positive even integer. The possibility of arbitrarily choosing both the number of arcs and the number of vertices of a network is considered in Problem 6.

A *path* in a network is a sequence of different arcs in the network that can be traversed continuously without retracing any arc. That is, each arc of the sequence must have one of its arc ends considered as the initial end and the other as the terminal end. The same vertex must be at the terminal end of the first arc and the initial end of the second arc; similarly, the terminal vertex of the second arc must be the initial vertex of the third arc, and so on. A vertex of an arc of a path is called a vertex of the path. The initial vertex of the first arc of a path is the *initial vertex* of the path; the terminal vertex of the last arc of a path is the *terminal vertex* of the path. A path is *closed* iff its initial and terminal vertices are the same point. Paths are sometimes designated by listing the succession of vertices along the path. Such a designation may be ambiguous; for example, there are 4 different paths in the network of Fig. 1.2 which could be designated by $ACBACD$. When an unambiguous notation is required, points which are not vertices are included to indicate exactly which arcs form the path under consideration.

Example 1.1 In Fig. 1.4, there are two different paths which are denoted by ABC; only one of these is denoted by $ADBC$.

Example 1.2 The path $ADBCA$ (Fig. 1.4) is made up of the arcs ADB, BC, and CA. The vertex A is both the initial and terminal vertex for the path;

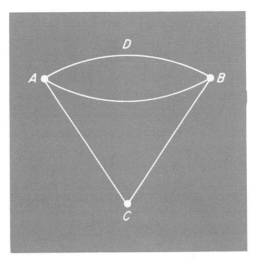

FIGURE 1.4

hence the path is closed. The vertex C is the terminal vertex of the arc BC and the initial vertex of the arc CA.

A network is *connected* iff every two different vertices of the network are vertices of some path in the network. The network shown in Fig. 1.3d is not connected; all the other networks in Fig. 1.3 are connected.

With this background, we can now prove some general results about networks from which it will be easy to answer the questions about the Königsberg bridges.

Theorem 1.1 In any network, the total number of odd vertices is even.

PROOF. Given any network, for each positive integer i, let n_i be the number of vertices of the network of order i; also, let N be the total number of odd vertices and let D be the total number of arc ends. The total number of odd vertices is the sum of the numbers of vertices of orders $1, 3, 5, \ldots$.

$$N = n_1 + n_3 + n_5 + \cdots.$$

(There are only a finite number of terms in the sum on the right, although the exact number will depend on the network being considered. This notation will be used here and in Section 2-3; no infinite series will be involved.) Similarly, the total number of arc ends is the sum of the numbers of arc ends at vertices of orders $1, 2, 3, \ldots$. The n_1 vertices of order 1 account for exactly n_1 arc ends; the n_2 vertices of order 2 account for $2n_2$ arc ends, and so on. Hence

$$D = n_1 + 2n_2 + 3n_3 + \cdots.$$

It follows that

$$D - N = 2n_2 + 2n_3 + 4n_4 + 4n_5 + \cdots,$$

so that $D - N$ is an even number. Also, D is an even number since each arc has exactly two ends. Since $N = D - (D - N)$, N is even«.

A path in a network is said to *traverse* the network iff every arc of the network is included in the path. A collection of several paths in a network traverses the network iff each arc of the network is included in exactly one of the given paths.

The question about the Königsberg bridges can now be phrased: Is there a path which traverses the network of Fig. 1.2? The next four theorems describe the conditions under which a network can be traversed by one, or several, paths.

Theorem 1.2 If a network has more than two odd vertices, it cannot be traversed by a single path.

PROOF. We shall prove the equivalent result: If a network can be traversed by a single path, then, with the possible exception of two of the vertices, each vertex of the network is even. Let $a_1, a_2, \ldots, a_n$ be a sequence of arcs forming a path which traverses a given network, and let A be any vertex of this network except the initial and terminal vertices of this path. The initial and terminal vertices of the path may coincide or they may be distinct. We shall show that A is an even vertex of the network. Imagine a point which starts at the initial vertex of a_1 and moves along a_1 to its terminal vertex (which is also the initial vertex of a_2), and then moves along a_2 to its terminal vertex (which is also the initial vertex of a_3), etc. until it finally arrives at the terminal vertex of a_n. Each time this point passes through the vertex A, it accounts for two arc ends at A — one on which to arrive and one on which to leave. Thus, the total number of arc ends at A must be even, and A is an even vertex of the network«.

Theorem 1.3 If a connected network has no odd vertices, then it can be traversed by a single path. Moreover, the initial vertex A_0 of the path can be chosen arbitrarily, and the first arc of the sequence forming the path can be chosen as any arc a_1 of the network having A_0 as one of its vertices.

PROOF. Given a network containing the arc a_1 with initial vertex A_0, let A_1 be the terminal vertex of a_1 (A_1 and A_0 might be the same point), and form a sequence of arcs in the network as follows: Let a_2 be any arc of the network different from a_1 and having A_1 as one of its vertices; take A_1 as the initial vertex of a_2 and let A_2 be its terminal vertex. Let a_3 be any arc of the network different from a_1 and a_2, and having A_2 as one of its vertices; take A_2 as the initial vertex of a_3 and let A_3 be its terminal vertex, and so on. This process, when continued as far as possible, produces a sequence $a_1, a_2, \ldots, a_n$ of distinct arcs which forms a path in the network. If the terminal vertex A_n of the arc a_n were different from the vertex A_0, the path $a_1, a_2, \ldots, a_n$ would account for an odd number of arc ends at A_n (two arc ends for each passage through A_n and one more as the terminal vertex of the arc a_n). Since every vertex of the network is even, there would be an arc of the network different from $a_1, a_2, \ldots, a_n$, and having A_n as one of its vertices, and the process could be continued. Thus, when the process is continued as far as possible, A_n must be the same as A_0 and the path $a_1, a_2, \ldots, a_n$ is closed.

If the path $a_1, a_2, \ldots, a_n$ traverses the entire network, the proof is complete; if not, since the network is connected, there is some arc b_1 different from $a_1, a_2, \ldots, a_n$, and such that one of the vertices B_0 of b_1 is a vertex of the path $a_1, a_2, \ldots, a_n$; say $B_0 = A_p$. Start again with the arc b_1, using B_0 as its initial vertex, and form a closed path consisting of a sequence $b_1, b_2, \ldots, b_m$ of arcs, each different from the others and also different from $a_1, a_2, \ldots, a_n$. Join the two closed paths into one by forming the sequence

$$a_1, a_2, \ldots, a_p, b_1, b_2, \ldots, b_m, a_{p+1}, \ldots, a_n.$$

The terminal vertex of a_p is the same as the initial vertex of b_1, and the terminal vertex of b_m is the same as the initial vertex of a_{p+1}, so this sequence is a path. If this enlarged path traverses the entire network, the proof is complete; if not, the path can be still further enlarged. Since there is only a finite number of arcs in the network, repeated enlargements must eventually produce a path which traverses the entire network (Problem 11 is concerned with the logical structure of this proof) «.

Theorem 1.4 If a connected network has exactly two odd vertices, it can be traversed by a single path whose initial and terminal vertices are the two odd vertices of the network.

PROOF. Given a network in which A and B are the only odd vertices, form a new enlarged network by joining A to B with a new arc a_0. In this enlarged network, every vertex is even; by Theorem 1.3, there is a path a_0, $a_1, \ldots, a_n$ which traverses this enlarged network. Then the path $a_1, a_2,$ $\ldots, a_n$ traverses the original network and the initial and terminal vertices of this path are the two odd vertices A and B «.

Theorem 1.5 If a connected network has exactly $2n$ odd vertices, it can be traversed by a collection of n paths and cannot be traversed by any collection containing fewer than n paths.

PROOF. Problem 3«.

PROBLEMS

1. (a) The problem of the Königsberg bridges was presented in connection with Figs. 1.1 and 1.2. Solve this problem.
   (b) There are nowadays nine bridges in Königsberg, as shown in Fig. 1.5

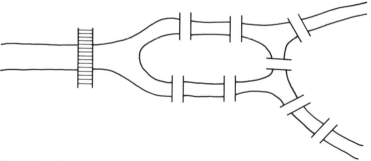

FIGURE 1.5

(one is a railroad bridge). Is it possible to make a walking tour of Königsberg which crosses each of these bridges exactly once? Can this be done if the railroad bridge is excluded?
   (c) Which of the networks in Fig. 1.3 can be traversed by a single path?

2. Figure 1.6 shows the floor plan of a five-room house. Is it possible to walk through each door exactly once?

3. Prove Theorem 1.5.

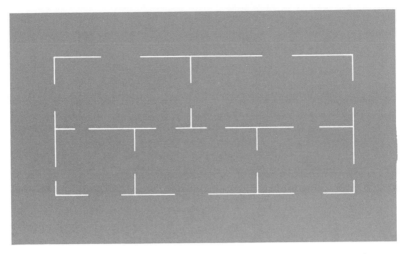

FIGURE 1.6

4. For each of the networks in Fig. 1.7 find a collection of paths which traverses the network and such that the network cannot be traversed by a collection of fewer paths. (Hint: First decide which points are vertices.)

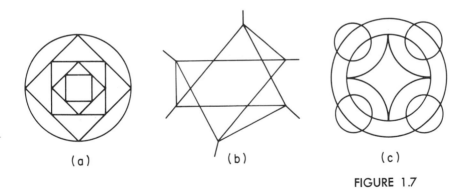

(a)   (b)   (c)

FIGURE 1.7

5. Prove that if a network has exactly 2 odd vertices then any path which traverses the network must have these two odd vertices as its initial and terminal vertices.

6. (a) Is there a network with 50 arcs and one vertex?
   (b) Is there a network with one arc and 50 vertices?
   (c) Find a network with five arcs and eight vertices.

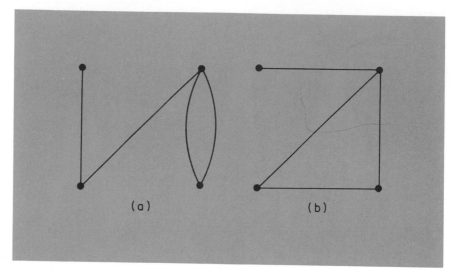

(a)　　　　　　　　　　　　　　　(b)

FIGURE 1.8

(d) Prove that, if n and m are positive integers such that $m \leq 2n$, then there is a network with n arcs and m vertices.

(e) Prove that, if n and m are positive integers such that $m \leq n + 1$, then there is a connected network with n arcs and m vertices.

7. **A chemical application.** The structure of a molecule can be schematically represented by a network. The vertices of the network represent the atoms of which the molecule is composed and the arcs represent chemical bonds between certain pairs of these atoms. Figure 1.8 shows two essentially different ways of forming a molecule with four atoms, two of which have two chemical bonds each, while the other two have one bond and three bonds, respectively.

(a) Prove that the molecules diagrammed in Fig. 1.8 are the only ones which can be formed from four atoms with the given bonds.

(b) Find three molecules which can be formed from four atoms, two of which have two chemical bonds each while the other two have three bonds each.

(c) Find four different molecules which can be formed from four atoms, two of which have three chemical bonds each, while the other two have two and four bonds, respectively.

8. **Hamiltonian paths.** The theorems of this article give necessary and sufficient conditions for a network to be traversable by a single path. A seemingly slight change in the properties desired of a path can completely change the complexity of the problem. A *Hamiltonian path* in a network is a closed path such that every vertex of the network is the terminal vertex of exactly one arc of the path (and consequently is also the initial vertex of exactly one

arc of the path). Necessary and sufficient conditions for a network to have a Hamiltonian path are not known. The problem originated with the Irish mathematician, Sir William Rowan Hamilton (1805-65) who discussed such paths along the edges of a regular dodecahedron.

(a) Which of the networks of Fig. 1.3 have a Hamiltonian path?

(b) Which of the networks of Fig. 1.7 have a Hamiltonian path?

9. (a) Explain why the theorems in Section 2-1 are of interest to a topologist.

(b) Find a theorem about networks which would not be of interest to a topologist.

10. (a) Explain how you decided which points were vertices in Fig. 1.7. Is the decision you made the only possible one?

(b) In a figure in which there is a point which may be a vertex but does not have to be a vertex, what is the order of this point if it is considered to be a vertex?

11. The proof of Theorem 1.3 is based on mathematical induction, but the inductive step is somewhat glossed over as the proof is presented in the text. Point out where this occurs in the proof and rewrite the proof with the inductive step formally presented.

2–2 Planar Networks

Each of the networks in the figures in Section 2-1 was drawn in a plane. In some cases, a network drawn in space may be topologically equivalent to a network in a plane. That is, it may be possible to find an elastic motion of a particular network in space which will place the network in a plane. Figure 2.1 shows a network in the plane which is topologically equivalent to the network of the edges of a tetrahedron. A network

FIGURE 2.1

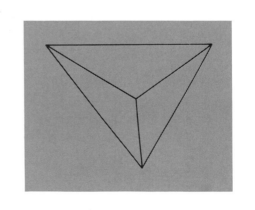

which is topologically equivalent to some network in a plane is called a
planar network. Thus Fig. 2.1 shows that the network of the edges of a
tetrahedron is planar. If the entire surface of a tetrahedron is to be considered, as well as the edges, it cannot be represented topologically by
Fig. 2.1, since, in that figure, a single point in the plane would represent
two points in different faces of the tetrahedron.

An interesting example of a non-planar network is the gas-water-
electricity network shown in Fig. 2-2. It shows the connections required
to supply each of three utilities (gas, water, and electricity, represented
by the points G, W, and E) to each of three houses (represented by the
points A, B, and C).

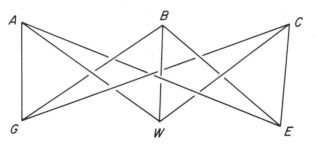

FIGURE 2.2

Theorem 2.1 The gas-water-electricity network is non-planar.

PROOF. We must show that no elastic motion of the network shown in
Fig. 2.2 will place this network in a plane. The proof is by contradiction.
Suppose there were such an elastic motion; then it would carry the
six arcs AG, GB, BW, WC, CE, and EA into a curve which completely
surrounds a portion of the plane (Fig. 2.3). Of the remaining three arcs,
AW, BE, and CG, one would have to be placed inside this curve and a
second one outside, and no matter how this is done, it is impossible to
place the last of the three arcs in the plane «.

A rigorous proof of Theorem 2.1 requires results about theta curves
which are beyond the scope of this text [*see* Ref. (28)].

Theorem 2.2 The network in which each of 5 vertices is joined by an arc
to each of the other 4 vertices (Fig. 2.4) is non-planar. This network is
called the complete network on 5 points.

PROOF. Problem 2 «.

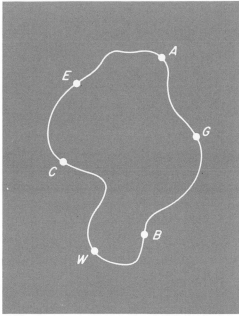

FIGURE 2.3

FIGURE 2.4

We have seen two examples (Figs. 2.2 and 2.4) of networks which cannot be placed in a plane. The Polish mathematician C. Kuratowski has used these two networks to characterize planar networks; his characterization also uses the concept of a subnetwork. A *subnetwork* of a given network is obtained by choosing any collection of paths in the given network subject to the following restrictions:

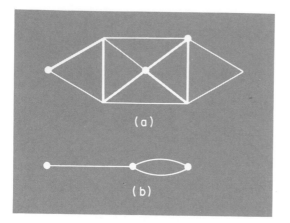

(a)

(b)

FIGURE 2.5

(1) No vertex is repeated along any one of the chosen paths (except that the initial and terminal vertices of a path may be the same).

(2) No two of the chosen paths intersect, except possibly at their initial or terminal vertices.

The chosen paths form the arcs of a new network, which is called a subnetwork of the given one. As an example, the network of Fig. 2.5b is a subnetwork of the one shown in Fig. 2.5a. It is obtained by choosing the paths which are shown by heavy lines in Fig. 2.5a. Of course, a network may have many subnetworks.

With this terminology we can present Kuratowski's result; he proved [Ref. (28)] that any network which cannot be placed in a plane must have a subnetwork which is topologically equivalent to the gas-water-electricity network or to the complete network on five points. Thus these two examples characterize planar and non-planar networks. The proof is beyond the scope of this text.

PROBLEMS

1. Which of the following networks are planar? For each one which is planar, find an elastic motion which will place it in a plane.
   (a) The edges of a cube.
   (b) The edges of a regular octahedron.
   (c) The edges of a regular dodecahedron.
   (d) The edges of a regular icosahedron.

(e) The legs, rungs, slats, perimeter of the seat, etc. of a chair.

(f) The edges and the diagonals of the faces of a cube. (Notice that the diagonals of any one face intersect; this intersection is, of course, a vertex.)

(g) The edges, the diagonals of the faces, and the body diagonals of a cube.

(h) The edges and body diagonals of a cube.

(i) The edges and body diagonals of a regular octahedron.

2. Prove Theorem 2.2.

3. Can the gas-water-electricity network (Theorem 2.1) be drawn on the surface of a sphere? On the surface of a doughnut?

4. Can the complete network on five points (Theorem 2.2) be drawn on the surface of a sphere? On the surface of a doughnut?

2–3 The Four Color Problem

How many colors do you need to color a map? No one knows for sure! We shall prove in this section that every map in a plane can be colored with five colors, but no one has found an example of a planar map which requires five colors — in each example that has been examined it has been possible to color the map with only four colors. Several excellent mathematicians have given considerable thought to this question, but nobody has been able to prove that four colors are always sufficient.

Before we begin the proof of the five color theorem, it will be necessary to understand very clearly what a planar map is, and what conditions are imposed on the coloring of a map. A *map* is a network, together with a surface which contains the network. If this surface is a plane, the map is called a planar map or a map in a plane; several examples are shown in Fig. 3.1. Only planar maps are considered in this section. Maps in more general surfaces will be discussed in Chapter 4.

The distinction between a planar network and a planar map may appear at first to be a minor one, but this is not the case. The entire viewpoint is changed; this change is emphasized by using, in connection with maps, notation and terminology which is somewhat different from that which we have used in our work on networks. The main interest in a network is focused upon the arcs of the network, with the vertices playing a subordinate roll. In a map, the main interest is centered on the portions into which the surface is divided by the arcs of the network, with the

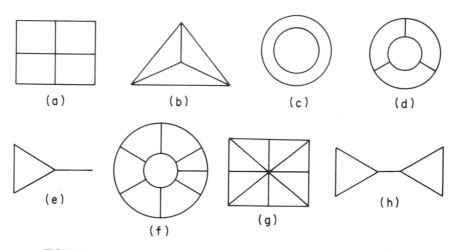

FIGURE 3.1   Examples of Maps in a Plane.

network itself playing a subordinate roll. In an ordinary map in an atlas, these portions of the surface are the states or countries shown by the map; in the general case, these portions of the surface are called the *faces* of the map. In an ordinary map in an atlas, we shall count the portion of the plane outside the map as one of the faces of the map; thus, in a plane, one of the faces of a map will be unbounded. The arcs and vertices of the network are called *edges* and *vertices* of the map, respectively; the edges which form the boundary of a particular face are called the edges of that face. Usually, the edges in a map are edges of two different faces, but Figs. 3.1e and 3.1h show that it is possible for an edge to be an edge of only one face.

In coloring a map, two faces which have an edge in common must be colored with different colors; if two faces have only vertices, or no boundary points in common, they may be colored the same color. For example in the map in Fig. 3.1a, the four quarters of the square could be colored with only two colors since the same color could be used for diagonally opposite quarters. The region exterior to the square would have to be colored a third color.

We are now ready to start toward the five color theorem. Several auxiliary results will be needed for the proof; the first of these results will also be useful in other situations. A map is *connected* iff the network of the map is connected. In any connected, planar map, there is a relationship among the numbers of vertices, edges, and faces of the map, as shown by the following theorem.

Theorem 3.1 (Euler) If V, E, and F are, respectively, the numbers of vertices, edges, and faces of a connected planar map, then $V - E + F = 2$.

PROOF. It is intuitively evident that any connected map in a plane can be built up by starting with a single edge and performing a succession of the following three operations.

    (i) Add a new edge joined at one end only;
        added: 1 vertex, 1 edge, no faces.

   (ii) Add a new vertex in an existing edge;
        added: 1 vertex, 1 cdgc, no faces.

  (iii) Add a new edge joined at both ends;
        added: no vertices, 1 edge, 1 face.

When we start with just one edge there are two possibilities; either there are two vertices and one face or there are only one vertex and two faces; in either case,

$$V - E + F = 2.$$

Now notice that none of the three operations described above makes any change in the sum $V - E + F$ since each adds one edge and either adds a vertex and no faces or adds a face and no vertices. Thus, with V, E, and F being, respectively, the number of vertices, edges, and faces in the completed map, we still will have

$$V - E + F = 2\text{«}.$$

A map is *regular* iff each vertex is of order 3. The maps shown in Fig. 3.1b and Fig. 3.1d are regular. In a regular, connected map, the following lemma shows that at least one face must be relatively simple.

Lemma 3.2 Any regular, connected map in a plane has at least one face with five or fewer edges.

PROOF. In a regular, connected map with V vertices, E edges, and F faces, let n_i ($i = 1, 2, 3, \ldots$) be the number of faces with i edges. Then the total number of faces is $n_1 + n_2 + n_3 + \cdots$ so that

$$n_1 + n_2 + n_3 + \cdots = F. \tag{1}$$

Second, each edge has exactly 2 ends, and there are exactly three arc ends at each vertex. Thus, each of the numbers $2E$ and $3V$ gives the total number of arc ends in the map, and these two expressions must be equal.

$$2E = 3V. \tag{2}$$

Third, each edge in the map is either an edge of only one face, or it is an edge of exactly two faces. Thus, if we find the number of edges in each face and add all these numbers, some edges may be counted once, and some twice, but no edge will be counted more than two times. The n_1 faces, each of which has one edge, account for n_1 edges; the n_2 faces, each of which has two edges, account for $2n_2$ edges, and so on; hence,

$$n_1 + 2n_2 + 3n_3 + \cdots \leq 2E. \tag{3}$$

By Theorem 3.1, we have

$$V - E + F = 2. \tag{4}$$

From Eqs. (2) and (4),

$$12 = 6V - 6E + 6F = 4E - 6E + 6F = -2E + 6F,$$

so $6F = 12 + 2E$. But this result, combined with Eqs. (1) and (3), gives

$$6n_1 + 6n_2 + 6n_3 + \cdots \geq 12 + n_1 + 2n_2 + 3n_3 + \cdots$$

or

$$5n_1 + 4n_2 + 3n_3 + 2n_4 + n_5 - n_7 - 2n_8 - \cdots \geq 12.$$

Since, for each i, the number of faces with i edges is either positive or zero, at least one of n_1 to n_5 must be positive; that is, there is at least one face with five or fewer edges «.

We can now prove a result of the type we have been expecting. It deals with the coloring of certain special maps in a plane, and six colors are allowed. Later, we will be able to reduce the number of colors to five, and remove the restrictions on the maps.

Lemma 3.3 Any regular connected map in a plane can be colored with six colors.

PROOF. The proof is by induction on the number of faces in the map. Any map with six or fewer faces can certainly be colored with six colors. Consider a regular connected map with n faces, $n > 6$, and suppose that every regular connected map with fewer than n faces can be colored with six colors; it will suffice to show that this map can be colored with six colors. By Lemma 3.2, there is at least one face f of this map which has five or fewer edges. At least one of the edges of this face must separate it from another face (Problem 1). Choose any such edge e and remove it from the figure; the two vertices at the ends of e thus become vertices of order 2, so, by joining two edges into one, they no longer need to be considered as vertices. Thus, the removal of the edge e joins f to another face and forms a new regular connected map with $n - 1$ faces. By the induction hypothesis, this map can be colored with six colors. When the edge e is replaced, to regain the original map, the face f will have an edge in common with at most five other faces, so there is sure to be at least one of the six colors available for the face f «.

PROBLEMS

1. Prove the statement made in the proof of Lemma 3.3, that at least one edge of f must separate f from another face. (Hint: Start with an arbitrary edge of f and form a path composed of edges of f; since the map has only a finite number of vertices, some vertex will have to appear twice in this path if it is continued far enough.)

2. In the proof of Lemma 3.3, what happens if the face f has only one edge, as shown in Fig. 3.2? (Hint: When the edge e is removed, the vertex to which it was attached becomes a vertex of order 1; is it possible to simultaneously remove the other edge attached to this vertex?)

3. For each of the maps shown in Fig. 3.1, what is the smallest number of colors with which it can be colored?

4. (a) For each of the regular connected maps shown in Fig. 3.3, find a face f, with five or fewer edges, and an edge e of f, such that e separates f from another face. Obtain a regular connected map which has one less face than the given map by removing the edge e, as explained in the proof of Lemma 3.3

FIGURE 3.2

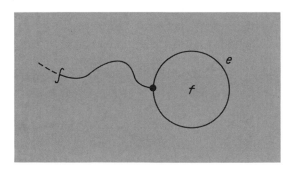

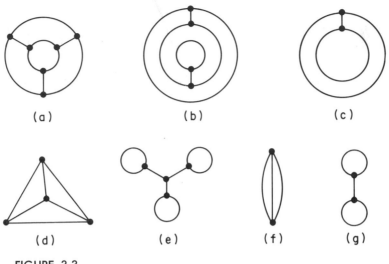

(a)   (b)   (c)

(d)   (e)   (f)   (g)

FIGURE 3.3

and in Problem 2 above. (Note: For the induction step in the proof of Lemma 3.3, we considered maps with more than six faces, but, for simplicity, the ones pictured in Fig. 3.3 have fewer faces.)

(b) The induction step in the proof of Lemma 3.3 cannot be performed with the maps shown in Figs. 3.3c, 3.3f, and 3.3g. Why does it fail for these maps? Prove that this induction step can be performed with any regular, connected, planar map having more than two vertices.

5. Prove that there cannot be more than five regular solids. (Hint: Consider the network of the edges of the solid. If each vertex is of order n and each face is a polygon with m sides, show that $nV = 2E = mF$, then use Euler's theorem.)

6. (a) Prove that in any regular connected map there are an even number of vertices.
(b) Prove that if n is any positive even integer, there is a regular connected map with n vertices.

7. In the proof of Lemma 3.3, why is the network still connected after the edge e is removed?

8. Draw a map in which no face has fewer than six edges.

Now that we have seen that six colors are sufficient to color any regular connected map, our next task is to show that the same result can be accomplished with only five colors.

Lemma 3.4 Any regular connected map in a plane can be colored with five colors.

PROOF. The proof is by induction on the number of faces in the map. Any map with five or fewer faces can certainly be colored with five colors. Consider a regular connected map with n faces, $n > 5$, and suppose that every regular connected map with fewer than n faces can be colored with five colors; it will suffice to show that this map can be colored with five colors. As in the proof of Lemma 3.3, there is at least one face f, with five or fewer edges, but here the proof breaks into three cases.

CASE 1. The face f has four or fewer edges. The proof continues exactly as for Lemma 3.3: Find an edge e of f which separates f from another face; remove e from the map to obtain a regular connected map with $n - 1$ faces; color this reduced map. When the edge e is replaced in the map, the face f will have an edge in common with at most four other faces, so there is sure to be at least one of the five colors available for the face f.

CASE 2. The map has an edge e (Fig. 3.4) such that when e is removed the map becomes disconnected. Since e disconnects the map, the same

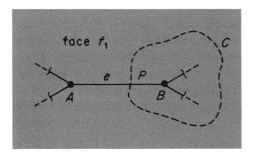

FIGURE 3.4

FIGURE 3.5

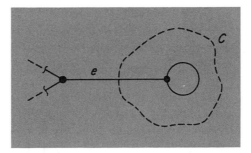

face f_1 must appear on both sides of e and, in this face, we may draw a curve C, such as the dashed curve in Fig. 3.4, which goes from one side of e to the other. If there is only one face of the map enclosed within C, then this face must have only one edge, as shown in Fig. 3.5, and this situation has been considered in Case 1. Similarly, Case 1 arises if there is only one face of the map which lies entirely outside C.

If there are at least two faces of the map inside C and at least two outside C, the original map can be replaced by two separate maps, as shown in Figs. 3.6a and 3.6b. These two maps are obtained by cutting the edge e at the point P (Fig. 3.4) where it intersects C, thus disconnecting the network; we consider the two maps formed by the separate pieces

FIGURE 3.6

of the network. Each of the two new maps is made regular by the addition of a loop at the point where e was cut. In Fig. 3.6a the face f_1 has been enlarged to include everything that was inside C in Fig. 3.4 (except for the new face inside the loop); similarly, the face f_1 in Fig. 3.6b includes almost everything that was outside C in Fig. 3.4. Now, in making each of these new maps, at least two faces of the original map were included in the face f_1, and only one new face was added by the loop, so each of these maps has fewer faces than the original map. By the induction hypothesis, each of these separate maps can be colored. Color them so that the face f_1 is the same color in the two maps; a coloring of the original map in Fig. 3.4 can be obtained by putting together the two maps of Fig. 3.6 and shrinking the loops to a point.

CASE 3. The removal of any one edge does not disconnect the map, and there is a face f with five edges. In this case no edge can have the same face on both sides of it, since its removal would then disconnect the map. Thus, the face f has five edges, as shown in Fig. 3.7, and each of the edges e_1, e_2, e_3, e_4, e_5 has a face different from f on the other side of it. Denote by f_i the face on the other side of e_i.

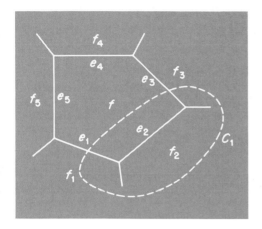

FIGURE 3.7

The faces f_1, f_2, f_3, f_4, f_5 may not all be different from each other, but we show next that at least two of them are different and, moreover, have no edge in common. In fact, if f_1 and f_3 have no edge in common, we may use them; if they do have an edge in common, then it is possible to draw, in the faces f, f_1, and f_3, a curve C_1 such as is shown dashed in Fig. 3.7. This curve completely encloses f_2 or completely encloses both f_4 and f_5; in either case f_2 can have no edge in common with f_5.

We now suppose that f_1 and f_3 are two faces which have no edge in common. Remove from the map both of the edges e_1 and e_3, making a new map in which the three faces f, f_1, and f_3 are joined into one, as shown in Fig. 3.8. The new map is kept regular by the usual suppression of vertices, and the removal of e_1 and e_3 leaves the map still connected be-

FIGURE 3.8

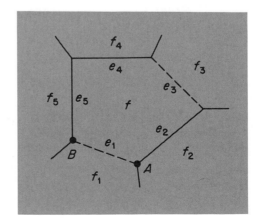

cause, for example, the points A and B may be joined by going around the edge of the old face f_1. This new map has two fewer faces than the original one; hence, by the induction hypothesis, the new map can be colored with five colors. But then the original map can also be colored with five colors, because, when the edges e_1 and e_3 are replaced, the faces f_1 and f_3, having no edge in common, can be allowed to remain the same color and there will be at most four different colors used for the five faces f_1, f_2, f_3, f_4, f_5, leaving at least one of the five colors available for the face f «.

It is now quite easy to prove the five color theorem; all that is needed is to remove the two restrictions of regularity and connectedness on the maps which are under consideration.

Theorem 3.5 Any map in a plane can be colored with five colors.

PROOF. First consider any connected map in a plane. We can obtain a regular connected map by "blowing up" each vertex which is of order $n \neq 3$ into a small face with n edges. Figure 3.9 illustrates the process

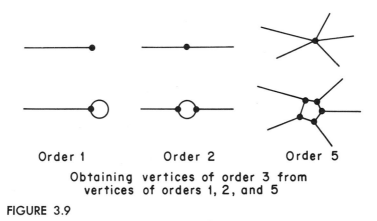

Order 1   Order 2   Order 5

Obtaining vertices of order 3 from
vertices of orders 1, 2, and 5

FIGURE 3.9

for vertices of orders 1, 2, and 5. Since, by Lemma 3.4, the resulting regular connected map can be colored with five colors, we can obtain a coloring of the original connected map merely by shrinking to a point each one of the small faces which were added. This shrinking process makes no change in the edges which are common to two different faces of the original map, so the coloring remains satisfactory. Therefore, any connected map in a plane can be colored with five colors.

Finally, consider an arbitrary map in a plane. If it is not connected, we may connect it by the addition of new edges in such a way that each of these new edges will have the same face on both sides of it. The preceding paragraph shows that the connected map can be colored with five colors, and we can obtain a coloring of the given arbitrary map by simply erasing the new edges which were added to connect the map. Since each of these new edges has the same face on both sides of it, the same color will appear on both sides of each of these edges, and the coloring will still be satisfactory after the edges have been erased «.

PROBLEMS (continued)

9. For each of the maps in Fig. 3.10, obtain a regular connected map by carrying out the construction suggested in the proof of Theorem 3.5.

10. (a) For each of the maps in Fig. 3.11, decide which of the cases of the proof of Lemma 3.4 apply. (The cases are not mutually exclusive, so more than one case may apply.)
(b) In each map (Fig. 3.11) a particular face with five edges is marked with the letter *f*. Try to carry out the procedure of Case 3, Lemma 3.4 with this face.

11. Figure 3.12 shows a regular connected map in a plane. Which cases in the proof of Lemma 3.4 apply to this map? Show that this map can be colored with four colors.

FIGURE 3.10

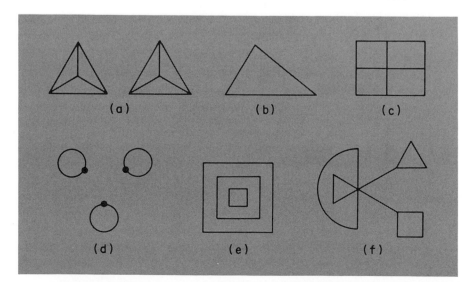

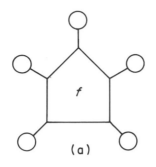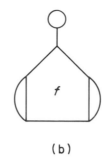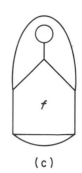

(a) (b) (c)

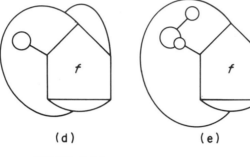

(d) (e) (f)

FIGURE 3.11

FIGURE 3.12

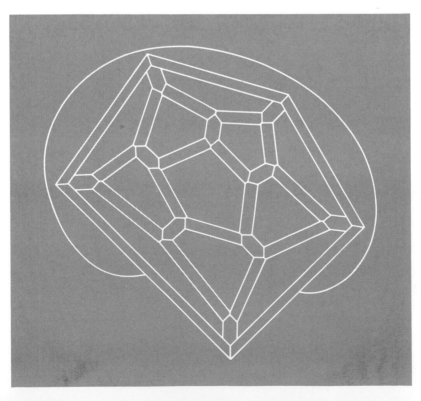

12. Prove the following statement made in connection with Fig. 3.4 in the proof of Case 2, Lemma 3.4: If there is only one face of the map enclosed within C, then this face must have only one edge.

13. Prove the following result, which was used in the proof of Case 3, Lemma 3.4: If an edge e of a map has the same face on both sides of it, then the removal of e will disconnect the map.

14. Prove the following statement made in connection with Fig. 3.8 in the proof of Case 3, Lemma 3.4: The points A and B may be joined by going around the edge of the old face f_1.

*15. Show that it is not possible to draw a map in a plane in which five of the faces have the property that each of them has an edge in common with each of the other four. Why doesn't this prove the four color theorem? (Hint: Remember that the complete network on five points cannot be drawn in a plane.)

16. Show by an example that, for any positive integer n, it is possible to have n solids in three-dimensional space, each of which has an area (face) in common with each of the others. Thus the immediate generalization of the four color problem to volumes in three-dimensional space is uninteresting.

THREE

Topological Equivalence
in
Three-Dimensional Space

3–1 Topological Equivalence

A solid ball is topologically equivalent to a solid
cube, or to any regular solid. As mentioned in
Chapter 1, two figures in three-dimensional
Euclidean space are called topologically equivalent iff there is an elastic motion which will make
one of the figures coincide with the other. Of
course, if we are presented with two physical
objects, one of which is a solid rubber ball and
the other a solid wooden cube, we cannot make
the rubber ball "coincide" with the wooden cube.
If we try to do so, they bump into each other and
the rubber ball flattens out against the outside of

the cube instead of moving on through the interior of the cube. This serves to emphasize the fact that the figures studied in mathematics — both in Euclidean geometry and in topology — are not physical objects but abstractions. A triangle is not a thing that can be made out of wood, paper, or string — it is composed of "line segments" which fit together in a certain way, and "line segments" are certain collections of "points." Thus, an adequate foundation for any serious study of either geometry or topology requires some discussion of sets of points, and a clear understanding of how one set of points is made to coincide with another. This foundation will be laid in Chapter 6; for the present, we shall continue to rely on an intuitive feeling for topological equivalence of figures based on the concept of an elastic motion of a perfectly elastic figure.

Several standard figures in which we shall be interested are described below. Some of them have appeared informally in our previous work, but their descriptions are included here for completeness.

A *circle* is a curve in a plane, all points of which are at a given distance from some particular point of the plane. The particular point is the *center* of the circle, and the given distance is the *radius* of the circle. A *simple closed curve* is a curve which is topologically equivalent to a circle. A simple closed curve may, or may not, lie in a plane. Figure 1.1 shows an example of a knotted simple closed curve which does not lie in a plane.

An *open disk* is the portion of a plane which is enclosed within some circle, but not including the circle. A *closed disk* is the portion of a plane which is inside or on some circle; that is, all the points of the circle are included in the closed disk. Note that both open and closed disks are surfaces in a plane. A closed disk is an open disk together with the circle whose interior is that open disk.

FIGURE 1.1

FIGURE 1.2

A *sphere* is a surface in three dimensions, all points of which are at a given distance from some particular point. The particular point is the *center* of the sphere and the given distance is the *radius* of the sphere.

An *open ball* is the portion of three-dimensional space which is enclosed within some sphere, but not including the sphere. A *closed ball* is the portion of three-dimensional space which is inside or on some sphere; that is, all the points of the sphere are included in the closed ball. Note that both open and closed balls are solids in three dimensions. A closed ball is an open ball together with the sphere whose interior is that open ball.

A *sphere with p handles* is a surface in three dimensions obtained by cutting $2p$ holes in a sphere and bending p different tubes so that their ends fit in these holes. Figure 1.2 shows a sphere with three handles.

A *torus* (Fig. 1.3) is a surface in three dimensions obtained by rotating a circle about a line which lies in the plane of the circle but does not intersect the circle. A torus may be thought of as the surface of an inner tube or of a doughnut. (*topologically equiv. to sphere with 1 handle*)

If two figures are topologically equivalent, we may be able to prove this fact by exhibiting an elastic motion which carries one of the figures

FIGURE 1.3

into the other. For example, given a rubber band in the shape of a circle, we could cut it, bend it into the shape of the curve of Fig. 1.1, and then fasten the two ends together as they were originally. This would prove that the curve of Fig. 1.1 really is a simple closed curve, since it is topologically equivalent to a circle.

How could we hope to prove that two figures are not topologically equivalent? It would be necessary to show that no elastic motion of one of the figures would make it coincide with the other figure. Of course, we cannot try each of the elastic motions in turn — there are too many of them. One way of giving such a proof is to find a property possessed by one of the figures which is lacking in the other figure. If this property is a topological property, the two figures cannot be topologically equivalent, because no elastic motion can either create or destroy this property, so no elastic motion can make one of the figures coincide with the other. We illustrate this procedure by proving that a sphere is not topologically equivalent to a torus. In fact, any simple closed curve on a sphere disconnects the sphere — if the surface is cut along any simple closed curve, the surface falls apart in two pieces. A torus does not have this property, since it is not disconnected by a circle going through the hole and around a cross section of the torus — if a torus is cut along such a circle, the surface becomes a tube, but it is still all in one piece. Moreover, the property of a surface's being disconnected by any simple closed curve lying in the surface is clearly a topological property. Thus, a sphere and a torus are not topologically equivalent.

PROBLEMS

1. (a) Prove that a torus is topologically equivalent to the surface of a button with one hole, and also to a sphere with one handle.
   (b) Is there a simple closed curve on a torus which disconnects the torus?

2. Prove that the surface of a button with p holes is topologically equivalent to a sphere with p handles.

3. (a) Prove that a sphere with two handles is not topologically equivalent to a sphere with three handles.
   (b) Prove that if $p \neq q$, a sphere with p handles is not topologically equivalent to a sphere with q handles.

4. Arrange the following items in groups so that all items in the same group are topologically equivalent, and items in different groups are not topologically equivalent.
   (a) A circle.
   (b) An open disk.
   (c) A line segment.
   (d) A sphere.

FIGURE 1.4

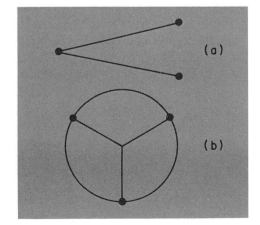

(e) A spherical shell (the portion of three-dimensional space which lies between two spheres which have the same center and different radii).

(f) A ball. *solid*

(g) The surface of a cube.

(h) A solid cube.

(i) A solid cube with a hole bored through it.

(j) A torus.

(k) The network composed of the edges of a tetrahedron.

(l) A solid in the shape of a piece of gas pipe.

(m) A solid in the shape of a piece of gas pipe together with a plug at each end.

(n) A solid in the shape of a heavy leather glove for the right hand.

FIGURE 1.5

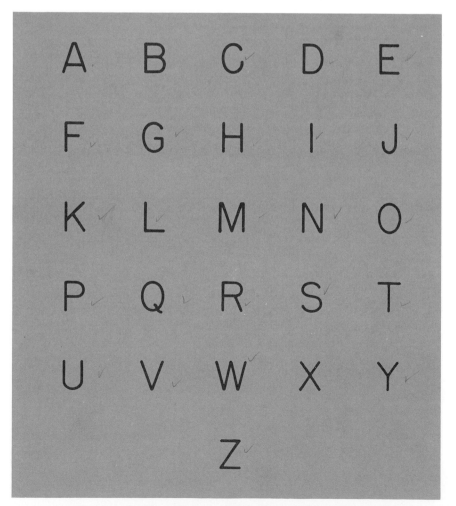

(o) A solid in the shape of a heavy leather glove for the left hand.

(p) A plain solid gold ring.

(q) An annulus (the portion of a plane which lies between two circles which are in that plane and have the same center and different radii).

(r) The entire surface of a phonograph record.

(s) The network of Fig. 1.4a.

(t) The network of Fig. 1.4b.

5. Block letters are shown in Fig. 1.5. Arrange the letters in groups, so that all the letters in the same group are topologically equivalent, and letters in different groups are not topologically equivalent.

3–2 Classification of Surfaces

Every schoolboy knows that an ordinary piece of paper has two sides; sometimes he must write only on one side, and sometimes he may write on both sides. In this section we shall see some examples of surfaces which have only one side, but first we must describe a little more in detail exactly what surfaces we are considering.

A surface should be "two-dimensional," like a plane or a sphere; but what about a sphere with a spine sticking out (Fig. 2.1a) or two tangent spheres (Fig. 2.1b); are these surfaces? In this section we consider a special type of surface called a manifold. A *manifold* is a connected surface (i.e., a surface "all in one piece") such that, sufficiently near to each point, the surface is topologically equivalent to an open disk. That is, for each point p of the surface, all of the points of the surface sufficiently near to p form a set topologically equivalent to an open disk. The set of all points of the surface near to p is called a neighborhood of p.

Neither of the surfaces shown in Fig. 2.1 is a manifold. In Fig. 2.1a, the points on the spine do not have satisfactory neighborhoods, and in Fig. 2.1b the surface is not topologically equivalent to a disk near the point of tangency of the two spheres.

A surface is *bounded* iff the entire surface is contained in some open ball. A torus is a bounded surface; a plane is not a bounded surface. If we consider a particular piece of a surface, the *boundary* of that piece is defined to be the curve which separates that piece from the rest of the surface. For example, consider a disk as a portion of a plane; the boundary of the disk is the circle which encloses it; the boundary of an annulus in a plane consists of two circles. Notice that the boundary of a piece

(a)

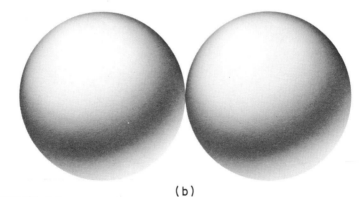

(b)

FIGURE 2.1

of a surface is not completely determined by that piece, but depends also
on the rest of the surface, since the boundary must be a "divider" or
"edge" between these two sets. An example will clarify this point. As
noted above, if we consider a disk as a piece of a plane, its boundary is a
circle. However, suppose we consider a disk as a piece of that disk itself;
then all the points of the surface are in the piece under consideration, so
certainly there is no "divider" between that piece and the rest of the
surface. That is, when the disk is considered as a subset of itself, it has no
boundary. We will have a more satisfactory definition of "boundary" in
Section 8-3; for the present we shall be interested only in simple cases, so
the intuitive concept will suffice. When we speak of the boundary of a
surface, we shall be considering that surface as a piece of some surface
which is a natural extension of it—for instance, a disk in a plane. It is

also important to notice that, although the words "bounded" and "boundary" are quite similar, the concepts are not at all similar. Both a sphere and a disk are bounded surfaces, but a sphere has no boundary, while the boundary of a disk is a circle. A plane is an unbounded surface which has no boundary; a thin strip of a plane is an unbounded piece whose boundary consists of two parallel lines. A surface is *closed* iff it is bounded and has no boundary. A sphere is a closed surface, since it is bounded and since one can move about freely on a sphere and never come to an edge. On the other hand, neither an open disk nor a closed disk is a closed surface, since each disk has as its boundary the circle which encloses the disk. Notice that the word "closed" is used here in connection with surfaces in a way similar to the way in which it was used in Section 2-1 in connection with paths in a network; in either case, it indicates that motion is never halted by an end or an edge. (The condition of boundedness was not required for a closed path, since all our paths were bounded.) A manifold may, or may not, be a closed surface. A sphere is a closed surface which is a manifold; an open disk is a manifold which is not a closed surface; a closed disk is not a manifold, since, near a point of the boundary circle, the surface is not topologically equivalent to an open disk.

There is an interesting way of representing certain manifolds as rectangles with some sides identified. For example, in Fig. 2.2 the ends of the rectangle are to be joined so that the two segments labelled AB coincide, with the two arrows pointing in the same direction. The manifold represented by this rectangle is the curved surface of a cylinder. Notice that the line segments BB and AA represent the two circles at the ends of the cylindrical surface. The points on these line segments (or circles) cannot be included in the manifold, since they do not have satisfactory neighborhoods on the surface. This representation of a cylinder

FIGURE 2.2

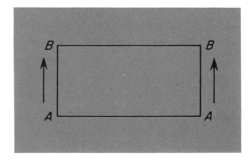

is sometimes convenient, since it will lie flat on a desk and all of one side of the surface can be seen at once.

Suppose that one of the arrows in Fig. 2.2 is reversed, as shown in Fig. 2.3a. If one end of this rectangle is given a half twist and the ends are then joined so that the two segments labelled AB coincide, with the two arrows pointing in the same direction, a manifold called a Möbius strip (Fig. 2.3b) is obtained. As with Fig. 2.2, the horizontal line segments at the top and bottom of Fig. 2.3a must be excluded from the surface to obtain a manifold. However, these line segments no longer represent two circles; here they represent two halves of the same simple closed curve. A Möbius strip has only one side. To see this, imagine a fly which starts at the point P and crawls along the curve C on the surface, returning to P along the dotted portion of C. Since the fly does not go through the surface, nor around the edge of the surface, it must be on the same side of the surface all the time. But it appears to return to the point P on the "other side" of the surface from where it started. Thus, what appear to be two different sides of the surface at P are really just two different pieces of the same side of the surface. Notice that one-sidedness is an extrinsic, rather than intrinsic, property of a surface. That is, the test as to whether or not a surface is one-sided is not carried out entirely on the surface, but instead use is made of the space around the surface. In our example with the fly, we have implicitly agreed that if the fly walks with his feet always on the surface, and does not cross any edge of the surface, then all the points through which his head moves must lie on the same side of the surface. If the surface is a Möbius strip, the fly can move his head from any point near the surface to any other point near the surface. Hence, all points are on the same side of the surface, and the surface is one-sided. Problems 5 through 9 are concerned with an intrinsic property of surfaces which is closely allied to one-sidedness.

FIGURE 2.3 Möbius Strip

(a)   (b)

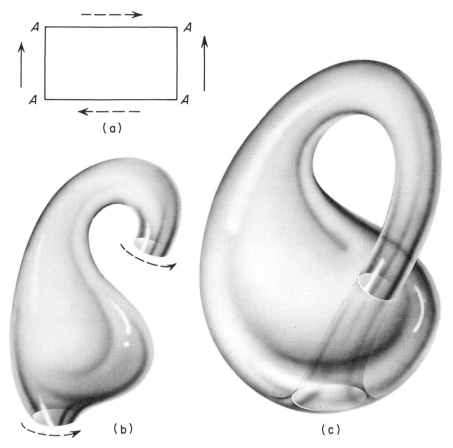

(a)

(b)

(c)

FIGURE 2.4 Klein Bottle

Another example of a one-sided surface is shown in Fig. 2.4. This manifold is called a Klein bottle, and it cannot be made in three-dimensional space. Figure 2.4a shows the representation of a Klein bottle as a rectangle with two pairs of edges identified. Identification of the two edges marked with the solid arrows gives a cylindrical surface (Fig. 2.4b), with the two ends of this cylinder still to be identified. This is the step which cannot be performed in three-dimensional space; one end of the cylinder must be thrust through the side and joined with the other end inside as shown in Fig. 2.4c. However, the surface must not intersect itself where the neck is thrust through the side (a fourth dimension is needed to "go around" the surface instead of through it).

The next theorem gives an interesting classification of closed two-sided manifolds. A similar classification of one-sided manifolds may be found in the references provided.

Theorem 2.1 Any closed two-sided manifold is topologically equivalent to a sphere with some number of handles.

PROOF. The proof of this theorem is beyond the scope of this book. The interested reader can find a proof in Ref. (8), Theorem 2, p. 33, or in Ref. (1), Theorem 7.2, p. 110«.

PROBLEMS

1. For each of the following surfaces tell whether it is (i) closed or not closed, (ii) a manifold or not a manifold, (iii) one-sided or two-sided, (iv) bounded

FIGURE 2.5

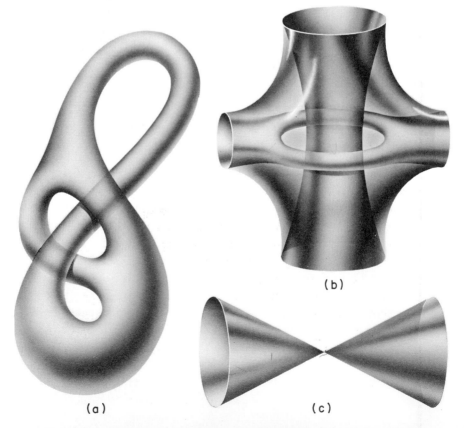

(a)

(b)

(c)

or unbounded. For each one which is a closed two-sided manifold, find the number p such that the surface is topologically equivalent to a sphere with p handles.

(a) A plane.
(b) A torus.
(c) A Möbius strip.
(d) A Klein bottle.
(e) An open disk.
(f) A closed disk.
(g) The surface of Fig. 2.5a.
(h) The surface of Fig. 2.5b.
(i) The portion of the conical surface with two nappes which is shown in Fig. 2.5c.
(j) The entire surface (rungs, slats, seat, back, etc.) of a chair.

2. What surface is represented by a rectangle with sides identified as shown in Fig. 2.6?

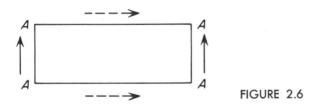

FIGURE 2.6

3. Experiment with the cylindrical surface and Möbius strip shown in Fig. 2.7 by twisting one end several times before attaching it to the other end, and then cutting the surface along the dotted curve C. What is the effect of the extra twists?

FIGURE 2.7

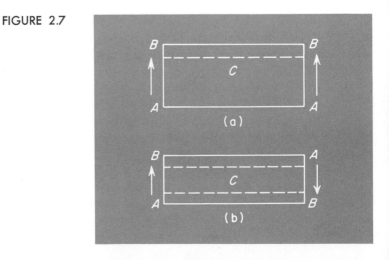

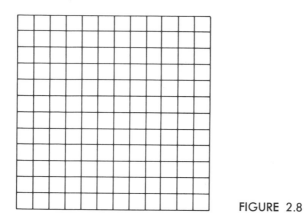

FIGURE 2.8

4. There is an old oriental game called Go-Moku or Five-in-a-row, which is played by two players using a square board ruled with 13 or 25 lines each way (Fig. 2.8). Each player has a supply of counters in his own color, and the players move alternately by putting a counter at one of the intersections on the board. The counters are never moved after they are placed. The first player to get five of his counters adjacent in a row (horizontal, vertical, or diagonal) wins. Play this game on a torus (Fig. 2.6) or a Klein bottle (Fig. 2.4a) ruled with about eight lines in each direction. Because the edges are identified, it will be more convenient to put the counters in the squares rather than on the intersections of the lines.

5. (**a**) Prove that on a Möbius strip it is possible to choose a direction of rotation about some point P, and then move P around on the surface without changing the direction of rotation about the moving point, but still arrange that when P has returned to its initial position the direction of rotation is different from that originally chosen. A surface which has this property is

FIGURE 2.9   FIGURE 2.10

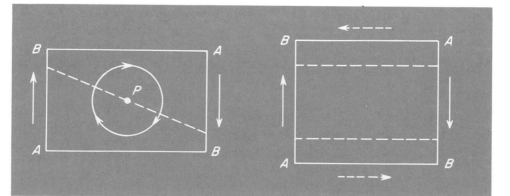

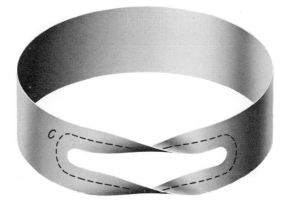

FIGURE 2.11

called *non-orientable*; otherwise the surface is *orientable*.   (Hint: Try moving *P* along the dotted curve in Fig. 2.9.)

(b) Is a torus orientable or non-orientable?

(c) Is a Klein bottle orientable or non-orientable?

6. The surface shown in Fig. 2.10 is a *projective plane*. It is topologically equivalent to a surface studied in courses in projective geometry, although in these courses it is usually approached from a somewhat different standpoint.

(a) Prove that a projective plane can be considered as a disk and a Möbius strip whose edges are joined.   (Hint: Cut the projective plane of Fig. 2.10 along the dotted line.)

(b) Is the projective plane orientable?

(c) Is the projective plane a manifold?

7. Prove that a manifold contained in ordinary three-dimensional space is orientable if and only if it is two-sided.   (Hint: Consider a fly walking on the surface and the motion of a right-hand screw from the fly's feet to his head.)

8. Is the surface shown in Fig. 2.11 a manifold?   Is it orientable or non-orientable?   What happens if the surface is cut along a curve which goes around the surface, staying just below the upper line in the drawing?   What happens if the surface is cut along the dotted curve *C*?

*9. Fig. 2.12 shows a solid cube of edge 2 units in length with its center at the origin. We identify pairs of points on the surface of this cube according to the following rule: On the faces $x = 1$ and $x = -1$, identify points which are symmetric with respect to the z-axis; i.e., identify $(1, y, z)$ and $(-1, -y, z)$. On the faces $y = 1$ and $y = -1$, identify points which

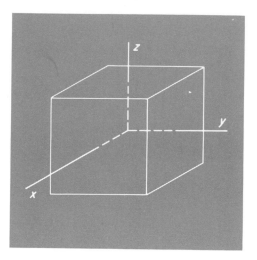

FIGURE 2.12

are symmetric with respect to the x-axis; i.e., identify $(x, 1, z)$ and $(x, -1, -z)$. On the faces $z = 1$ and $z = -1$, identify points which are symmetric with respect to the xy-plane; i.e., identify $(x, y, 1)$ and $(x, y, -1)$.

We now have a solid in which, for each point, all of the space near that point is topologically equivalent to a ball. Such a solid is called a three-dimensional manifold. However, this three-dimensional manifold is peculiarly twisted. Consider the three surfaces obtained as the intersections of this solid with the three coordinate planes.

(a) Which of these surfaces is orientable?

(b) Which of these surfaces is one-sided in this solid? (Hint: Imagine a fly walking with his feet on the surface, and find out where it is possible for his head to go.)

(c) Similarly, discuss the surface composed of all the points whose coordinates satisfy the equation

$$x^2 + y^2 + z^2 = \tfrac{1}{4}.$$

Maps on a Sphere with Handles

4–1 Introduction

In Section 2-3 we defined a map as a network together with a surface which contains the network, and we discussed some properties of maps in a plane. In Chapter 3 we discussed more general surfaces and stated that any closed two-sided surface is topologically equivalent to a sphere with some number of handles. In this chapter we shall discuss maps on these more general surfaces. Since the four color problem in the plane is still unsolved, it might be suspected that very little would be known about coloring maps on these more general surfaces.

Surprisingly enough, the map-coloring problem has proved to be easier on these more general surfaces. The solution to the map-coloring problem on a torus is presented in Section 4-4.

4–2 Simply Connected Sets

In any map on a given surface, the faces of the map are the separate pieces into which the surface is divided by the arcs of the network of the map. Thus any face of a map is a connected piece of a surface. Such a connected piece is called *simply connected* iff every simple closed curve in that piece can be deformed into a point in the piece; that is, during the deformation the curve must remain in the piece.

Figure 2.1a illustrates the fact that a disk is a simply connected set; any simple closed curve C, in the disk, can be deformed into a point in the disk. On the other hand, an annulus, or ring-shaped region (Fig. 2.1b), is not simply connected, since the curve C cannot be deformed into a point without leaving the region. A plane and a sphere are also examples of simply connected sets; a torus is not simply connected. Notice that the deformation of a curve into a point is not an elastic motion because distinct points of the curve are made to coalesce into the same point.

Of course, even in a connected set which is not simply connected, there may be some simple closed curves which can be deformed into a point in the set. If there were some way to change the set so that only

FIGURE 2.1

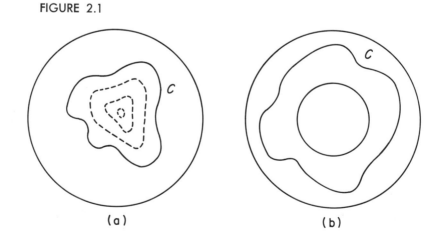

(a)   (b)

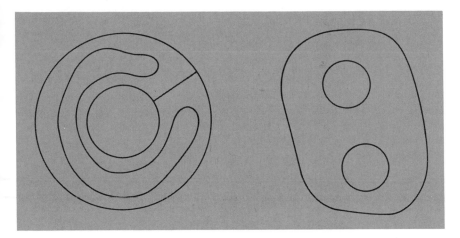

FIGURE 2.2   FIGURE 2.3

those simple closed curves were still available, the set could be changed into a simply connected one. The usual way to make this change is to remove certain arcs from the set. These arcs which are removed are called *cuts*. Figure 2.2 shows a simply connected set obtained by making one cut in the annulus of Fig. 2.1b. With the points of this cut removed from the annulus, any simple closed curve in the set can be deformed into a point in the set.

There are connected sets (Fig. 2.3) in which two cuts are required to make the set simply connected. It is easy to see how to obtain sets which require three, four, or any larger integral number of cuts to make them simply connected.

It is not really obvious that every connected set can be changed into a simply connected one by making certain cuts in the set. The difficulty is that a simply connected set must be connected, and it is conceivable that the cuts needed to make the set simply connected might separate the set into two or more pieces. We shall assume that any face of a map on a closed two-sided surface can be made simply connected by cuts.

For the sets in Figs. 2.1 and 2.3, it is easy to see that after the cuts have been introduced to make the surface simply connected, any additional cut will disconnect the surface; that is, any additional cut will separate the surface into two pieces. We shall assume the following result: On a closed two-sided manifold, any cut in a simply connected set separates the set into two simply connected pieces.

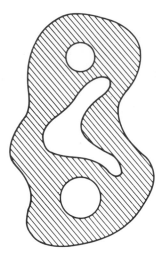

FIGURE 2.4

PROBLEMS

1. Which of the following surfaces are simply connected?   Make cuts in each
   one which is not simply connected so that it becomes simply connected, and
   check that any additional cut would separate the surface into two simply
   connected pieces.
   (a) A torus.
   (b) A sphere.
   (c) A sphere with two handles.
   (d) The portion of a sphere shown in Fig. 2.4.
   (e) Each face of the map on a sphere with three handles shown in Fig. 2.5.

FIGURE 2.5

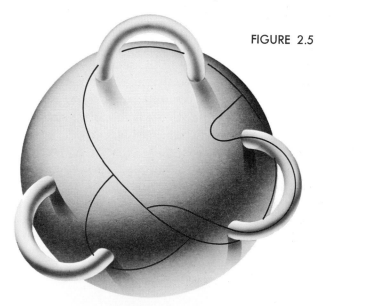

4-3 Euler's Theorem

In this section we shall prove Euler's theorem (Theorem 3.3) for the general case of a sphere with p handles. It is convenient to consider first the sphere itself (i.e., with no handles), and to use Euler's theorem in the plane (Theorem 3.1 in Chapter 2) to obtain the result for the sphere. There are several ways in which maps on a sphere can be correlated with maps in a plane. One of the simplest such correlations is given by a polar projection, which is shown in Fig. 3.1. The plane is tangent to the sphere at the point S, and the point N is diametrically opposite to S; that is, N and S are the end points of a diameter of the sphere. For any point P on the sphere, and different from N, the line through N and P intersects the plane in exactly one point Q. Conversely, for each point Q in the plane, the line through N and Q intersects the sphere in exactly one point P which is different from N. Thus we have a correspondence between points on the sphere and points in the plane. The point S on the sphere corresponds to the same point S in the plane. The point N on the sphere does not correspond to any point in the plane, but N is the only point on the sphere with no corresponding point in the plane. This point-to-point correspondence is called the *polar projection* from N, and the point N is called the *pole* of the projection,

Any map on a sphere can be transferred to a plane by choosing any point N of the sphere, which is not on the network of the map, and using

FIGURE 3.1 Polar projection of a sphere onto a plane

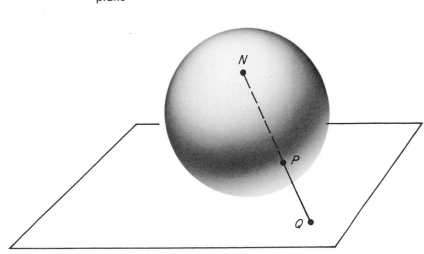

the polar projection from N. Conversely, any map in a plane can be transferred to a sphere by a polar projection, and the pole of the projection will not be on the network on the sphere. In fact, the pole will always be in the face which corresponds to the "outside" face of the map in the plane.

Theorem 3.1 (Euler) If a connected map on a sphere has V vertices, E edges, and F faces, then

$$V - E + F = 2.$$

PROOF. Any connected map on a sphere can be transformed, by a polar projection, into a connected map in a plane and the two maps will have the same numbers of vertices, edges, and faces. The result now follows from Theorem 3.1 in Chapter 2 **«**.

We have frequently made use of the fact that a circle, or any simple closed curve in a plane, separates the plane into three pieces — the piece inside the curve, the piece outside the curve, and the curve itself. Any simple closed curve on a sphere also separates the sphere into three pieces — two areas and the curve itself — but there is a difference in the two cases. In the plane a simple closed curve can be deformed into a point in the area inside the curve, but cannot be deformed into a point in the area outside the curve. On the sphere, a simple closed curve can be deformed into a point in each of the two areas of the remainder of the sphere. These facts are illustrated in Fig. 3.2. Incidentally, this result shows that a sphere and a plane are not topologically equivalent, since we have found a topological property in which they differ — not a very surprising result.

FIGURE 3.2

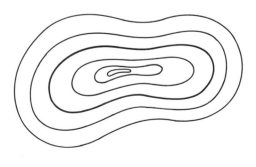

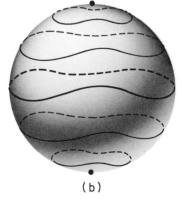

(a)   (b)

Another interesting result which can be obtained from these considerations is given in the following theorem.

Theorem 3.2 Each face of a map on a sphere is simply connected if and only if the map is connected.

PROOF. Given any map on a sphere in which the face f is not simply connected, we prove that the map is not connected. In fact, there is a simple closed curve C lying entirely inside f (C contains no points of the network), and C cannot be deformed into a point in f. Now if C is removed from the sphere, there remain two areas A_1 and A_2 of the sphere, and since C can be deformed into a point in either one of these regions, it follows that neither A_1 nor A_2 can be completely contained in f. Let us denote by A_i either of the areas A_1 or A_2. We have shown that A_i contains points of f and also points of some other face of the map; hence A_i must contain a portion of the network forming the boundary between two faces. But if any point on a particular arc of the network lies in A_i, the entire arc must lie in A_i, because the boundary curve C of A_i contains no points of the network. Thus A_i contains an entire arc of the network and must, therefore, contain a vertex of the network. Let a_i be a vertex of the network contained in A_i ($i = 1, 2$). No path in the network has both a_1 and a_2 as vertices, since such a path would have to cross C, and this proves that the network is not connected.

The proof of the converse is left as an exercise (Problem 3) **«**.

Theorem 3.2 shows that for connected maps on a sphere, the faces are simply connected; the same result is not true of connected maps in a plane, nor is it true of connected maps on a sphere with p handles ($p > 0$). However, Euler's theorem can be extended to maps on a sphere with handles if the hypothesis that the map is connected is replaced by the requirement that each face be simply connected.

Theorem 3.3 (Euler) If a map on a sphere with p handles has V vertices, E edges, and F faces, and if each face is simply connected, then

$$V - E + F = 2 - 2p.$$

PROOF. Before beginning the proof we make two preliminary comments.

First, notice that the equation we are to prove expresses a topological property of the map. In proving this result we are free to change the map by any elastic motion, and, if we can demonstrate that the equation is correct for the changed map, it must also be correct for the original map. Some of the elastic motions we shall use in the proof will leave the entire surface in the same shape and position, but will stretch or shrink certain faces of the map so that some individual points will be moved to a different place on the surface. We shall describe these elastic motions as "sliding the network around on the surface" but, of course, in the actual elastic motion, the surface must slide along with the network.

Second, notice that we may alter the map (the network or the surface) in any way we wish so long as we arrange that, for the new map (with V' vertices, E' edges, and F' faces), the sum $V' - E' + F'$ has the same value as $V - E + F$; in fact, we can even permit an alteration in the map for which

$$V' - E' + F' \neq V - E + F,$$

provided that we keep track of the change in the value of this expression and allow for it in our final result.

We are now ready to give the proof of Theorem 3.3; it is illustrated in Fig. 3.3 for the case of a sphere with three handles. Only a portion of the network is shown in the figure. We consider (Fig. 3.3a) any map with simply connected faces, on a sphere with p handles, and suppose that the network has been slid around so that there is no vertex on any one of the circles in which the handles join the sphere, and so that none of these circles has a segment in common with any arc of the network. Since each face of the map is simply connected, no single face can contain a circular cross section of one of the handles. Thus, for each handle, there must be at least one path in the network which goes along that handle lengthwise. (Figure 3.3a shows two such paths for the handle h_1 and one path for each of the handles h_2 and h_3.)

We now make three successive changes in the map, for each of which

$$V' - E' + F' = V - E + F.$$

First, for each handle h_i, we choose one of the circles C_i in which that handle joins the sphere, and we add new vertices to the network by placing a vertex at each intersection of the network with any of the circles C_i ($i = 1, 2, \ldots, p$). Each of these added vertices divides an arc into two smaller arcs, so if we let n be the number of new vertices which are added to the network, then also the number of edges is increased by n; no change is made in the number of faces.

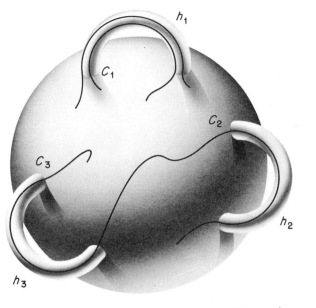

(a)

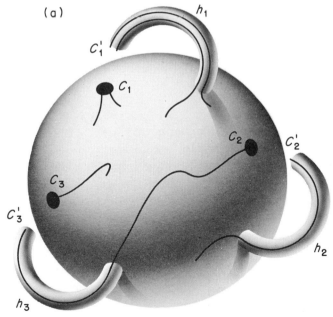

(b)

FIGURE 3.3(a) & (b)

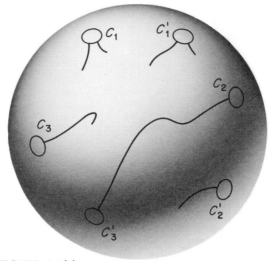

FIGURE 3.3(c)

(c)

Second, we add new arcs to the network by placing an arc along each one of the pieces into which any one of the circles C_i is divided by the new vertices which were added in the first change above. On each of the circles C_i, the number of arcs added in this second step is the same as the number of vertices added in the first step; thus, the total number of arcs added is n. Each of these arcs is a cut in one of the simply connected faces of the map, so each new arc divides a face into two smaller simply connected faces, making a total increase of n in the number of faces; no change is made in the number of vertices.

Third, we cut the surface along each of the circles C_i and pull the cut end of each handle slightly away from the sphere so that the handles become tubes sticking out from the spherical surface (Fig. 3.3b). At the same time, we alter the network by duplicating the vertices and arcs of C_i on the cut end of the handle h_i. This copy of C_i is denoted by C'_i. A total of n vertices, n edges, and no faces have been added to the map in the third step. The surface is now a sphere with p circular holes cut in it and with p open-ended tubes sticking out of the surface. There are now $V + 2n$ vertices, $E + 3n$ edges, and $F + n$ faces in the map.

Finally, we make a change in the map for which

$$V' - E' + F' \neq V - E + F;$$

we pull each of the tubes back onto the surface, obtaining a sphere with $2p$ circular holes cut out of it, and we fill up these holes by adding to the map $2p$ faces in the form of open disks (Fig. 3.3c). We now have a map on a sphere with $V + 2n$ vertices, $E + 3n$ edges, and $F + n + 2p$ simply connected faces. By Theorem 3.2, this final map on a sphere is connected; hence, by Theorem 3.1,

$$(V + 2n) - (E + 3n) + (F + n + 2p) = 2$$

or
$$V - E + F = 2 - 2p \text{«.}$$

PROBLEMS

1. Consider the polar projection of the earth in which the pole N is the North Pole.
   (a) What are the images in the plane of the circles of latitude on the sphere?
   (b) What are the images in the plane of the circles of longitude on the sphere?
   (c) What are the images in the plane of the circles on the sphere which are neither circles of latitude nor circles of longitude?
   (d) Characterize the curves on the sphere whose images in the plane are straight lines.

2. Find a (non-connected) map on a sphere for which $V - E + F \neq 2$. What values of $V - E + F$ are possible for maps on a sphere?

3. Prove that if each face of a map on a sphere is simply connected, then the map is connected.

FIGURE 3.4

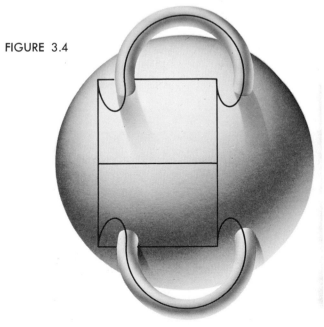

4. (**a**) Prove that no map in a plane has all of its faces simply connected.
   (**b**) Show by an example that, for any $p > 0$, there is a connected map on a sphere with p handles, in which one of the faces is not simply connected.

5. Figure 3.4 shows a map on a sphere with two handles.
   (**a**) What are the values of V, E, and F for this map?
   (**b**) Is each of the faces simply connected?
   (**c**) Show that it is impossible to slide the network of this map around so that, for each of the two handles, one of the circles in which it joins the sphere is made up of arcs of the network.
   (**d**) Referring to the proof of Theorem 3.3, show that for some maps the first two changes made in the map could be replaced by a single sliding of the map on the surface, but show that this cannot be done for all maps.

FIGURE 3.5

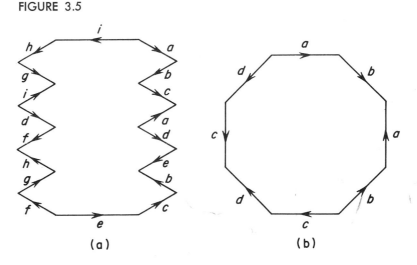

(a)   (b)

FIGURE 3.6

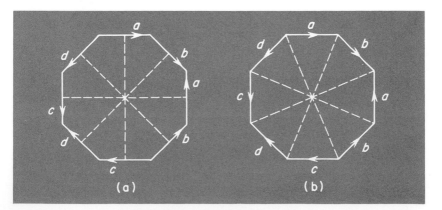

(a)   (b)

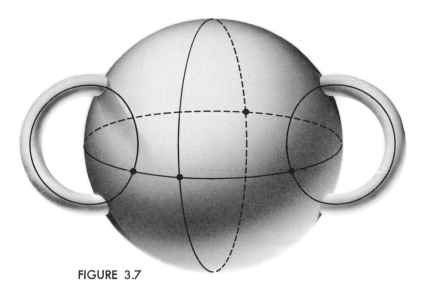

FIGURE 3.7

6. In Section 3-2 we found that a torus, which is topologically equivalent to a sphere with one handle, can be represented by a rectangle with the edges identified in a certain way. Show that either Fig. 3.5a or Fig. 3.5b represents a sphere with two handles. (Hint: Cut Fig. 3.4 along the arcs of the network to obtain Fig. 3.5a; simplify the map of Fig. 3.4 and cut again to obtain Fig. 3.5b.) In each of these figures, two sides labelled with the same letter are to be identified, with the arrowheads matching in direction.

7. Each of Fig. 3.6a and Fig. 3.6b represents a map on a sphere with two handles (only the dashed lines are edges of the map). Sketch each of these maps in a form similar to Fig. 3.4.

8. Each of Fig. 3.4 and Fig. 3.7 shows a map on a sphere with two handles. Represent each of these maps in a form similar to Fig. 3.6.

4–4 The Seven Color Theorem on a Torus

In Section 2-3 we proved that any map in a plane could be colored with five colors, and we mentioned that no planar map had so far been discovered which actually required five colors. Thus, for maps in a plane, the minimum number of colors which would suffice for any map is not exactly known. The discussion of polar projection in Section 4-3 showed that maps could be transferred from a plane to a sphere, or from a sphere to a plane. This means that the map-coloring problem on a sphere must be in exactly the same state of completion as the problem in the plane. Paradoxically, if we turn to a more complicated surface, such as the torus, the problem is completely solved.

Theorem 4.1 Any map on a torus can be colored with seven colors, and there is at least one map on a torus which requires seven colors.

PROOF. The construction of an example to show that seven colors may actually be required is left as an exercise (Problem 1).

The general outline of the proof that seven colors are sufficient is quite similar to that of the five color theorem (Theorem 3.5 in Chapter 2 and the Lemmas which precede it), and we shall omit some of the details.

First, we may confine our attention to maps in which the faces are simply connected, for, if we are given a map on a torus in which some of the faces are not simply connected, we may change the map by introducing cuts in such a way that all of the faces become simply connected. If this changed map can be colored with seven colors, a satisfactory coloring of the original map can be obtained by merely erasing the cuts.

Second, we may confine our attention to regular maps with simply connected faces because any vertex which is not of order 3 can be expanded into a small open disk (which is simply connected) and, if this new map can be colored with seven colors, so can the original map.

Third, every regular map on a torus, in which each face is simply connected, has at least one face with six or fewer edges. In fact, if the map has V vertices, E edges, and F faces, with n_i of the faces having i edges each, then

$$n_1 + n_2 + n_3 + \cdots = F.$$

Also, the total number of arc ends is given by $2E$ and by $3V$; hence

$$2E = 3V.$$

By Theorem 3.3

$$V - E + F = 0.$$

Since each arc of the network is an edge of at most two faces

$$n_1 + 2n_2 + 3n_3 + \cdots \leq 2E.$$

Eliminating V, E, and F from these relations gives

$$5n_1 + 4n_2 + 3n_3 + 2n_4 + n_5 - n_7 - 2n_8 - \cdots \geq 0.$$

Thus at least one of n_1 to n_6 must be positive.

Fourth, except in trivial cases, each face of a map on a torus has at least one edge which separates that face from a different face.

Fifth, and finally, the proof can now be completed by induction on the number of faces in the map. If there are seven or fewer faces, the result is obvious. Suppose that every regular map on a torus, with k simply connected faces, can be colored with seven colors, and consider any regular map on a torus with $k + 1$ simply connected faces. Choose a face f of this map with six or fewer edges, and choose an edge e of f which separates f from a different face. Remove the edge e, keeping the map regular by the usual suppression of vertices; this change in the map gives a regular map with k simply connected faces. By the induction hypothesis, this map can be colored with seven colors; when the edge e is replaced to regain the original map, there is sure to be at least one color available for the face f, because the faces which have an edge in common with f account for at most six colors «.

PROBLEMS

1. Give an example of a map on a torus with seven faces, each of which has an edge in common with each of the other six. Prove that seven colors are required to color this map. The torus may be represented by a rectangle with edges identified as in Fig. 2.6 in Chapter 3.

2. (a) Prove that, except in trivial cases, each face of a map on a torus has at least one edge which separates that face from a different face. What are the trivial exceptions?
   (b) Prove that when the edge e is removed from the map as described at the end of the proof of Theorem 4.1, each of the k faces of the new map is simply connected.

3. Carry out the steps in the proof of Theorem 4.1 for the maps on a torus shown in Fig. 4.1. The torus is represented as a rectangle with edges identified, and the network of the map is shown in dashed lines.

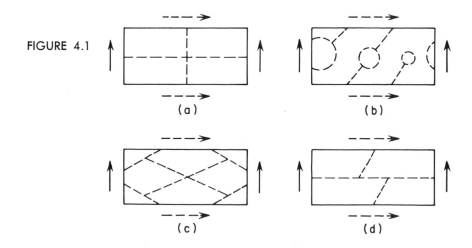

FIGURE 4.1

(a)   (b)   (c)   (d)

The

Jordan Curve Theorem

5–1 Introduction

The Jordan curve theorem is an important and frequently used result in topology; we have used it several times in our previous work. It states, roughly, that there are an inside and an outside of a simple closed curve in a plane. More exactly, if a simple closed curve C lies in a plane, and if the points of C are removed from the plane, the remainder of the plane is composed of exactly two connected pieces and the curve C is the boundary of each of these pieces. Intuitively, it is impossible to get from one of these pieces to the other in the plane without crossing the curve C.

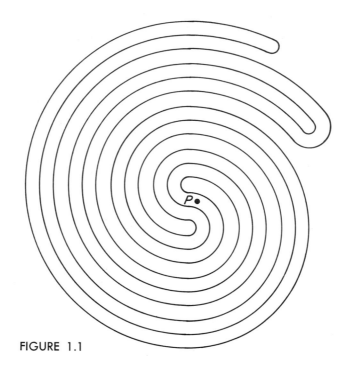

FIGURE 1.1

The result certainly seems evident for a circle in a plane, and it seems
equally plausible that any elastic motion will leave the portions of the
plane inside and outside of the curve still connected, and that these portions will still have the curve as their common boundary. However, let
us look at an example. Figure 1.1 shows a simple closed curve in a plane;
is the point P inside or outside this curve? Of course, it would be possible
to draw a much more complicated simple closed curve than the one
shown in Fig. 1.1. How can we be sure that we can always tell whether a
particular point, not on such a curve, is inside the curve or outside the
curve? Is there some test we could apply? The proof of the Jordan curve
theorem in its full generality is beyond the scope of this book, but a proof
is given in the next section for the special case of a polygon.

5–2 A Proof for the Case of a Polygon

Before proving the Jordan curve theorem for the special case of a polygon,
we must be quite sure that we understand exactly what a polygon is.

Let a_1, a_2, ... , a_n be a sequence of n points in a plane. There may be some repetition among the points, but it is required that each pair of points a_i, a_{i+1} which are adjacent in the sequence be distinct, so that they determine a unique line segment. The *polygonal path* with vertices a_1, a_2, ... , a_n is the sequence of $n - 1$ line segments a_1a_2, a_2a_3, ... , $a_{n-1}a_n$. The path is said to *join* the points a_1 and a_n. If the points a_1 and a_n are distinct, the *polygon* with vertices a_1, a_2, ... , a_n is the sequence of n line segments a_1a_2, a_2a_3, ... , $a_{n-1}a_n$, a_na_1. These line segments are the *sides* of the polygon. A polygon is *simple* iff all of its vertices are distinct and no two of its sides intersect except (possibly) at their end points.

We can now state the special case of the Jordan curve theorem which we shall prove.

Theorem 2.1 (Jordan) If S is any simple polygon in a plane P, the points of P which are not on S can be divided into two sets A and B in such a way that any two points in the same set can be joined by a polygonal path not intersecting S, while no two points, one of which is in A and the other in B, can be so joined.

PROOF. Choose a direction in the plane P which is not parallel to any side of the polygon S and, for each point x of the plane, denote by H_x the half line in the chosen direction starting at x. That is, H_x is the collection of all points on the line through x parallel to the chosen direction and lying on the side of x which is indicated by that direction. This process is illustrated in Fig. 2.1. Now let A be the set of all points x of the plane, not on S, for which H_x intersects S an even number of times. Similarly, let B be the set of all points, not on S, whose half lines have an odd number of points of intersection with S. In counting the number of intersections of a half line with S, there is a special rule for counting intersections at

FIGURE 2.1

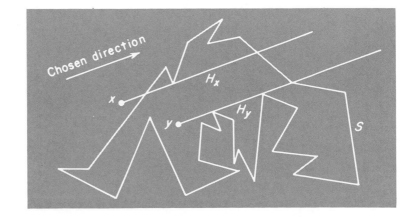

vertices of S. If the polygon crosses the half line at the vertex, this intersection is counted, but if the polygon does not cross the half line at the vertex, the intersection is not counted. Thus, in Fig. 2.1, H_x has two points of intersection with S, while H_y has only one point of intersection.

Now, if a point x moves along a line segment which does not intersect S, the number of intersections of H_x with S can change only when H_x moves past a vertex of S. But consideration of the two cases — (1) S crosses H_x at the vertex and (2) S does not cross H_x at the vertex — shows that, although the actual number of intersections of H_x with S may change, this number of intersections cannot change from even to odd nor from odd to even. Thus all points along any line segment (and hence along any polygonal path) not intersecting S are in the same one of the sets A or B. This proves that no point of A can be joined to a point of B by a polygonal path.

We have left to show that if p and q are any two points, either both in A or both in B, then p and q can be joined by a polygonal path not intersecting S. Consider the line segment pq (Fig. 2.2). If this line segment does not intersect S, it is a satisfactory path. If it does intersect S, form a polygonal path as follows: Go along the line segment pq until just before its first intersection with S, then go along line segments near to the sides of S (but do not cross S) until you are near the last intersection of pq with S. Proceed to q along a portion of the segment pq. The proof that this polygonal path does not intersect S is left as an exercise (Problem 2) **«**.

FIGURE 2.2

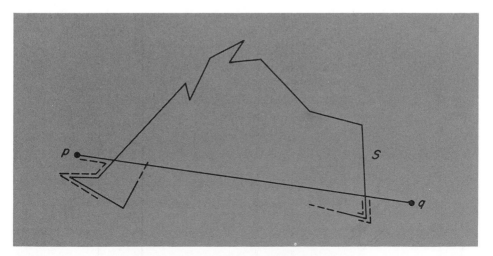

PROBLEMS

1. Which of the figures drawn in Fig. 2.3 represent polygonal paths? Which represent polygons? Which represent simple polygons? In each case, tell which points are vertices; is it possible to choose different vertices for the same figure?

FIGURE 2.3

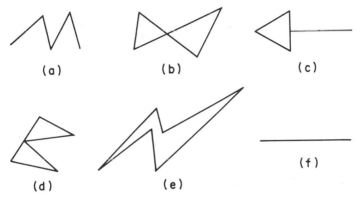

(a)   (b)   (c)

(d)   (e)   (f)

2. (a) Prove that S does not intersect the polygonal path constructed at the end of the proof of Theorem 2.1. (Hint: By the first part of the proof, all points along this path must lie in the same one of the sets A and B.)
   (b) For the sets A and B of Theorem 2.1, prove that there is at least one point in A and at least one point in B.

3. Is the statement and proof of Theorem 2.1 topological? Why or why not? Discuss.

4. What difficulties would you encounter in attempting to extend the proof of Theorem 2.1 to apply to an arbitrary simple closed curve?

5. (a) Define the inside and outside of a simple polygon.
   (b) Is the inside of a simple polygon simply connected? How about the outside?

6. In the proof of Theorem 2.1, the division of points between the sets A and B was based on counting certain intersections. Think of another property which might have been used to divide the points of the plane not on S into two sets with the desired properties.

SIX

Sets

6–1 Introduction

In several places in our work so far we have had occasion to consider collections of objects — perhaps all the points on a certain surface, or all the paths in a certain network. In the future, we shall be much more concerned with collections, or sets, of objects. We shall need some acquaintance with the notation and terminology used in connection with sets, as well as an intuitive concept of what constitutes a set. In the last part of the nineteenth century, some very serious questions arose in connection with the foundations of set theory; even today, not all of these questions have been answered to everyone's satisfaction. At least, everyone is agreed that the formation of sets must be somehow restricted or carried on by some sort of orderly process. Frequently, membership in a set is taken as one of the undefined concepts in a logical development of set theory. Certain axioms are stated which set membership is required to satisfy and other concepts are defined in terms of this one.

In this introductory text, we propose to ignore the restrictions on the formation of sets, except for brief references in some of the problems, and we shall develop our set theory intuitively rather than deductively. For the interested student, references to more rigorous developments of set theory are given in the bibliography [for example, Ref. (20)].

6–2 Relations Involving Sets

Everyone is familiar with sets or collections. A library is a collection of books; a committee is a set of people; a year is a collection of days; a galaxy is a set of solar systems. We shall use the terms set, collection, family, and aggregate as synonyms and shall think of a set as being composed of identifiable, distinguishable objects. That is, given any object whatever we must be able to identify or recognize this object, and from this recognition it must be possible to determine whether the object is an element of the set or is not an element of the set. Moreover, two objects which appear as different elements in a set must be distinguishable, one from the other; we do not allow identical objects to appear as different elements of a set. More simply, no repetitions are allowed among the elements of a set.

As an example, let us consider the set of all positive integers less than or equal to 10. In asserting that this is a set, we are maintaining that:

(1) Having given any object whatever, it can be determined whether this object is, or is not, a positive integer less than or equal to 10.

(2) Having given an object a, which is a positive integer less than or equal to 10, and an object b, which is a positive integer less than or equal to 10, it is possible to determine whether a is different from b, or whether the objects a and b are, in fact, identical.

At first glance, it may appear evident that the two determinations called for in (1) and (2) above can always be made, but carelessness in the making of these decisions is a fertile source of fruitless arguments. Let us look at another example: Suppose we are concerned with the set of all round objects and someone suggests the earth as an object for our consideration. Is the earth an element of our set or not? It is commonly said that the earth is round, but everyone knows that there are mountains, hills, and valleys on the earth; thus, the decision turns on the exact meaning to be attributed to the word "round." Another example: Suppose you lend a friend of yours a dime, which he promises to repay, and the next day your friend gives you ten pennies. Did your friend repay the debt? Are the ten pennies your friend gave you the same object as the dime you gave to him? Again we see that, in order to understand a statement, it is necessary to have a clear understanding of the meanings of the terms involved in the statement.

We shall generally use capital Roman letters to stand for sets, and lower case Roman letters for the elements of a set. If the object a is an element of the set A, we write

$$a \in A.$$

If the object a is not an element of the set A, we write

$$a \notin A.$$

There are two systems of notation which are in general use for naming sets. The first of these notations is most convenient in connection with a set which has only a few elements. In that case, the elements may be listed and enclosed between braces. For example, $\{0, 1\}$ is the set which has exactly two elements — the numbers 0 and 1. This listing of all the elements of a set makes it easy to decide, about any object, whether or not that object is an element of the set. It suffices to compare the object with each of the set elements in the list. If the object is identical with one of the elements in the list, it is an element of the set; otherwise, it is not. Of course, it still must be possible to determine whether or not two objects are identical. Consider the object $\frac{2}{2}$. Is it an element of the set $\{0, 1\}$? We recognize that "$\frac{2}{2}$" and "1" are just different names for the same object, so $\frac{2}{2} \in \{0, 1\}$.

If a set has many elements, or an infinite number, a complete listing of the elements of the set is impractical or impossible. In such cases, it may be possible to list a few of the elements of the set and expect the reader to guess correctly what the other elements are, either from the context, or from previous experience. For example, the set $\{3, 4, 5, \ldots, 498\}$ should be understood to have exactly 496 elements. These elements are all of the integers from 3 to 498 inclusive. Similarly, $\{1, 2, 3, \ldots\}$ is the set of all positive integers.

The second notation which may be used to name a set consists of a description of the set; that is, a test is given which can be applied to any object and such that, from the result of the test, it can be determined whether or not the object is an element of the set. A skeleton form for this notation is $\{x: \ldots\}$. The three dots are to be replaced by a statement of the test which any object x must pass in order to be an element of the set. For instance, $\{x: 3 \leq x \leq 498\}$ (which may be read "the set of all objects x such that x is between 3 and 498 inclusive") is composed of all the objects x (and no others) for which the statement $3 \leq x \leq 498$ is true. Thus, the essential feature of this second notation is that it tells how to determine, about any object, whether or not that object is an element of the set. For this second notation, just as with the first notation, the reader is sometimes required to supply, from context or otherwise, a part of the information which is not actually written down. For example, in a discussion of the integers, the set

$$\{x: 3 \leq x \leq 498\}$$

would be understood to have exactly the same elements as the set

$$\{3, 4, 5, \ldots, 498\}.$$

If the discussion was concerned with real numbers, these two sets would not have the same elements; e.g.,

$$\pi \in \{x: 3 \leq x \leq 498\}, \quad \text{but} \quad \pi \notin \{3, 4, 5, \ldots, 498\}.$$

A set which is named using the first notation discussed above is said to be *listed*; if the second notation is used, the set is said to be *described*.

Another way of looking at a description of a set is to notice that the three dots in the skeleton $\{x: \ldots\}$ are replaced by the statement that x possesses a certain property. The set is composed of all objects which actually do possess this property (and no others). The set

$$\{x: x \text{ is round}\}$$

is composed of all objects which are round. Thus, any property, such that each object either has this property or fails to have it, can be used to describe a set. Conversely, for any set there is a property which can be used to describe it. Clearly, if we are given a particular set A, the property of being an element of A is characteristic of its elements; i.e.,

$$A = \{x: x \in A\}.$$

This last equation raises the question of what we mean by saying that two sets are equal. We have said that a set is composed of the objects which are its elements. Thus it is natural to agree that two sets are equal if and only if they have the same elements.

Besides equality, there is another important relation between sets. If every element of a set A is also an element of the set B, we say that A is a *subset* of B, or A is *included* in B, and write $A \subset B$ or, equivalently, $B \supset A$. (We shall follow the convention of using "is contained in" in the sense of "is an element of" and "is included in" in the sense of "is a subset of.") As usual, the negation of $A \subset B$ is written $A \not\subset B$. Notice that each set A is a subset of itself, for surely every element of the set A is also an element of A! If $A \subset B$ and $A \neq B$, we say that A is a *proper subset* of B. If the sets A and B are given by descriptions, say

$$A = \{x : S(x)\}$$

and
$$B = \{x : T(x)\},$$

it is easy to see that $A = B$ if and only if, for all x, statement $S(x)$ is equivalent to statement $T(x)$; moreover, $A \subset B$ if and only if, for all x, statement $S(x)$ implies statement $T(x)$. Thus a study of the relations of equality and inclusion between sets is, at the same time, a study of equivalence and implication between sentential functions (functions whose values are sentences).

There are several special sets in which we shall be interested. It is frequently convenient to consider a set which contains all of the objects which it is necessary to consider in connection with a given problem. Such a set will frequently, but not always, be denoted by X and will be called the *universal set*, although the article "the" is somewhat misleading. If a universal set X has been chosen for a particular problem, any set which includes X could be used as the universal set for that problem. Of course, two different investigations may have completely different universal sets. The selection of a universal set may be thought of as a definition of the term "object"; it is understood that the definition is applicable only in connection with a particular investigation. In most cases, an acceptable universal set will be clear from the context, but where confusion seems likely, the universal set will be mentioned.

The second of the interesting special sets is far removed from the universal set. As we have noticed, any property of objects, such that each object either possesses this property or fails to possess it, gives rise to a set — namely, the set of all objects with the given property. But consider the property of being different from itself; no object possesses this property, since each object is identical with itself. Thus the set which is described by this property; that is, the set $\{x : x \neq x\}$ has no elements. From our definition of equality of sets, there is only one set which has no elements. It is called the *empty set* (null set, void set), and we shall reserve the symbol $\emptyset$ for this set. Notice that $\emptyset$ is a subset of every set A since each element of $\emptyset$ (there are none!) is also an element of A.

The sets which have exactly one element play an important role in many problems. Such sets are called singletons; the set $\{a\}$, whose only element is the object a, is called *singleton a*. It is important to notice that the object a and the set singleton a are not identical. That is, we conceive of the process of set formation as making a new object, different from the objects on which the process operates. This is evident for sets with more than one element — no one would confuse the set $\{a, b\}$ with the single object a — however, some confusion is possible between $\{a\}$ and a. That it is convenient, or even necessary, to distinguish between the two can be seen by considering the case in which the object under consideration is itself a set, say the set N of all positive integers. Then N has an infinite number of elements, whereas $\{N\}$ has only one; certainly, they cannot be the same.

The example just discussed shows that sets are themselves objects, and may appear as elements of other sets; thus we will not always be able to use the convention that capital Roman letters represent sets and lower case Roman letters represent elements of sets. For example, we may wish to consider a set of people, perhaps the set

$$\mathcal{T} = \{x : x \text{ is a person more than 6 feet tall}\}.$$

Each of the elements of $\mathcal{T}$ is a human being and may, therefore, be considered as a collection of molecules. Similarly, each of these molecules is a set of atoms. Thus we see that the elements of a set may themselves be rather complicated sets. On the rare occasions when this phenomenon is of interest to us, we shall try to use an appropriate notation, such as

    a, b, x, etc.:   Elements of the simplest type considered.

    A, B, S, X, etc.: Sets of elements such as a, b, x, etc.

    $\mathcal{A}, \mathcal{B}, \mathcal{S}$, etc.:   Collections of sets such as A, B, etc.

In connection with the set $\mathcal{T}$ of tall people described above, c might be a particular atom of carbon which, together with certain other atoms, forms a set which is a molecule M. A collection of such molecules could be a particular basketball player $\mathcal{B}$ and a suitable aggregate of basketball players would form a squad $\mathcal{S}$.

Example 2.1 Let

$$A = \{1, 2, 3\}$$

and $\qquad B = \{x : x \text{ is an integer} \quad \text{and} \quad 1 \leq x \leq 10\}.$

Then $A \subset B$ and $A \neq B$; hence A is a proper subset of B. Also $2 \in A$, $2 \not\subset B$, $\{2\} \not\subset A$, $\{2\} \subset A$. One description of A is given by

$$A = \{x : x \in B \quad \text{and} \quad -5 < x < 4\}.$$

Example 2.2 Let $A = \{1, 2, 3\}$ and $B = \{x : x \subset A\}$. Then

$$A \in B, \quad \text{but} \quad A \not\subset B;$$

$$1 \in A, \quad \text{but} \quad 1 \not\subset B;$$

$$\{1\} \not\subset A, \quad \text{but} \quad \{1\} \subset A \text{ and } \{1\} \in B.$$

The set B consists of eight elements; a listing of B can be given as

$$B = \{\emptyset, \{1\}, \{2\}, \{3\}, \{2, 3\}, \{1, 3\}, \{1, 2\}, \{1, 2, 3\}\}.$$

Example 2.3 The set $A = \{1, 1, 2, 2, 2\}$ has exactly two elements, 1 and 2.

PROBLEMS

1. Let $A = \{1, 2, 5, 9\}$.
   (a) Find an object which is an element of A.
   (b) Find an object which is not an element of A.
   (c) Find an object which is a subset of A.
   (d) Find an object which is not a subset of A.
   (e) Is there an object which is both an element and a subset of A?

2. Let $A = \{x : x \text{ is round}\}$ and $B = \{x : x \text{ is red}\}$.
   (a) Explain how you could determine, by examining an object, whether or not it is an element of A.
   (b) Find an object x such that $x \in A$ and $x \in B$.
   (c) Find an object y such that $y \in A$ and $y \not\in B$.
   (d) Find an object z such that $z \not\in A$ and $z \not\in B$.
   (e) Find a set C such that $C \subset A$ and $C \subset B$.

3. Each of the following sets is named by being listed. Give a description of each of these sets. Can you think of different descriptions for the same set? Which notation seems more natural and convenient?
   (a) $\{2, 3, 5, 7, 11, 13\}$.
   (b) $\{2, 3, 5, 7, \ldots\}$.
   (c) $\{1, 4, 9, 16\}$.
   (d) $\{1, 4, 9, \ldots, 625\}$.
   (e) $\{a, b, c\}$.
   (f) $\{a, b, \ldots, z\}$.
   (g) $\{$John Jones, Mary Smith$\}$.
   (h) $\{$the gas station on the corner of 1st and Main, the gas station on the corner of 2nd and Main$\}$.
   (i) $\{$Fig. 3.1 in Chapter 2, Fig. 7.9 in Chapter 2, Fig. 4.2 in Chapter 5$\}$.
   (j) $\{$the fourth word on the third line of page 17 of this book, the third word on the fourth line of page 27 of this book$\}$.

4. Each of the following sets is named by a description. Give a listing of each of these sets. Can you think of different listings for the same set? Which notation seems more natural and convenient?
   (a) $\{x: x \text{ is an integer} \quad \text{and} \quad x < 5\}$.
   (b) $\{x: x \text{ is an integer} \quad \text{and} \quad x > 5\}$.
   (c) $\{x: x \text{ is an integer} \quad \text{and} \quad 4 < x < 5\}$.
   (d) $\{x: x \text{ is an even integer}\}$.
   (e) $\{x: x \text{ is an even integer} \quad \text{and} \quad x \text{ is a prime}\}$.
   (f) $\{x: x \text{ is a word which begins with zy}\}$.
   (g) $\{x: x \text{ is a word which begins with s}\}$.
   (h) $\{x: x \text{ is a word which ends with pt}\}$.
   (i) $\{x: x \text{ is a word used in this book}\}$.
   (j) $\{x: x \text{ is the publisher of this book}\}$.

#5. Prove that $A = B$ if and only if $A \subset B$ and $B \subset A$. This result is the basis for many proofs of equality between sets.

6. Which of the following listings or descriptions names a set? Justify your answer by discussing whether or not it can be determined that an arbitrary object is, or is not, an element of the set. Mention any additional assumptions you are making from context, previous experience, or otherwise.
   (a) $\{$house, dog$\}$.
   (b) $\{$you, I$\}$.
   (c) $\{a, b, \ldots, Y, Z\}$.
   (d) $\{a, b, \ldots, 7, 8\}$.
   (e) $\{a, b, \ldots\}$.
   (f) $\{x: x \text{ is big}\}$.

(g) $\{x\colon x$ is a digit which appears in the decimal expansion of $\pi\}$.
(h) $\{x\colon x$ is a digit which appears between the 1,000,000th and the 2,000,000th decimal place in the decimal expansion of $\pi\}$.
(i) $\{x\colon x$ is a digit which is repeated infinitely often in the decimal expansion of $\pi\}$.
(j) $\{x\colon x$ is zybnatious$\}$.

7. How many subsets are there of the set

$$A = \{1, 2, \ldots, n\}?$$

How many of these are proper subsets?

8. Which pairs of the following objects are connected by one or more of the relations $=$, $\in$, $\subset$, or $\supset$?

$R = \{x\colon x$ is a real number$\}$.
$E = \{x\colon x$ is an even integer$\}$.
$F = \{x\colon x$ is a rational number$\}$.
$T = $ The number 2.
$V = \{x\colon x \in E$ and $x \notin R\}$.
$S = \{2\}$.
$D = 7 - 5$.
$\mathfrak{S} = \{x\colon x \subset F\}$.
$Q = \{x\colon x$ is a quotient of two elements of $E\}$.
$N = \{1, 2, 3, \ldots, n\}$.

9. Explain why $\emptyset$ is a subset of every set. Is $\emptyset \subset \emptyset$? Is $\emptyset \in \emptyset$?

10. Suppose that you were engaged in a project to prove the Pythagorean theorem. What would you choose for a universal set?

11. As we have seen, the elements of a set may be any objects whatever; in particular, these elements may themselves be sets. Thus it is conceivable that a set might contain itself as a member. Let us call a set "extraordinary" if it *does* contain itself as a member, and "ordinary" if it does *not* contain itself as a member. Set

$$\mathfrak{S} = \{x\colon x \text{ is an ordinary set}\}.$$

Prove that $\mathfrak{S}$ is neither ordinary nor extraordinary. This is one form of the Russell Paradox, first given by the British mathematician Bertrand A. W. Russell (1872-   ) in 1908. It shows that, if sets are to behave in the way in which our intuition would like, we must place some restriction or regulation on the formation of sets so that they do not become "too big." The appropriate restrictions on set formation are not discussed in this introductory text.

6–3 Operations Involving Sets

In the preceding section we have seen several relations which may hold between two sets or between an object and a set. In this section we shall consider ways in which sets may be used to manufacture other sets. Usually, two sets will be combined to produce a third set; such a procedure, or rule of combination, is called a binary operation. Binary operations are already familiar in other contexts — for example, either addition or multiplication of numbers is a procedure for combining two numbers to produce a third number. In fact, two of the set operations we shall define will have many properties in common with addition and multiplication of numbers. We shall also be interested in a unary operation by which a single set can be used to form another one.

Before we define these operations, it will be convenient to have available a schematic representation for sets. One such representation is by means of Venn diagrams in which (Fig. 3.1) the universal set is represented by the set of points enclosed within a rectangle, and the elements of a particular set A are represented by the points enclosed by a simple closed curve inside the rectangle. In the diagram, the point a represents an object which is an element of A: $a \in A$; similarly, the object represented by the point b is not an element of A: $b \notin A$.

The set operations can now be defined, and illustrated by Venn diagrams.

The *union* of two sets A and B, denoted by $A \cup B$, is the set (shaded in Fig. 3.2) defined by

$$A \cup B = \{x: x \in A \quad \text{or} \quad x \in B\}.$$

Notice that the word "or" is used in mathematics in the inclusive sense. That is, "statement S or statement T" means that at least one of the

FIGURE 3.1   FIGURE 3.2

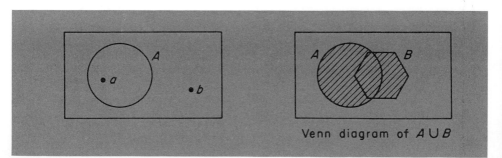

Venn diagram of $A \cup B$

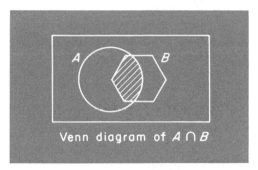

Venn diagram of $A \cap B$

FIGURE 3.3

statements S and T is true. Thus the condition "$x \in A$ or $x \in B$" means that the object x is an element of at least one of the sets A and B, and it may be an element of both of these sets. Of course, an object which is an element both of A and of B will appear only once as an element of $A \cup B$, since the same object cannot be repeated as two different elements of a set.

The *intersection* of two sets A and B, denoted by $A \cap B$, is the set (shaded in Fig. 3.3) defined by

$$A \cap B = \{x : x \in A \quad \text{and} \quad x \in B\}.$$

The operation of intersection can be used to define an important relation between sets. The sets A and B are said to be *disjoint* (or either one of the sets is disjoint from the other) iff $A \cap B = \emptyset$; that is, iff no object is an element of A and also an element of B. Two sets which are not disjoint are said to *meet*. We have already seen several examples of disjoint sets. The inside and outside of a simple closed curve in a plane are disjoint. If the faces of a map are thought of as the pieces of the surface obtained by removing the network from the surface, that is, if the edges of a face are not included in that face, then any two different faces of a map are disjoint.

In Section 8-3 we shall need somewhat more general operations of union and intersection than those defined above. If $\mathcal{Q}$ is any family of sets, we define the union of the family $\mathcal{Q}$ by

$$\cup \{A : A \in \mathcal{Q}\} = \{x : \text{There is an } A \in \mathcal{Q} \quad \text{with} \quad x \in A\}.$$

Similarly, the intersection of a non-empty family $\mathcal{Q}$ of sets is defined by

$$\cap \{A : A \in \mathcal{Q}\} = \{x : \text{For every } A \in \mathcal{Q}, \quad x \in A\}.$$

In case $\mathcal{Q} = \{A_1, A_2, \ldots, A_n\}$, we also write

$$\cup_i A_i \quad \text{and} \quad \cap_i A_i$$

in place of

$$\cup \{A : A \in \mathcal{Q}\} \quad \text{and} \quad \cap \{A : A \in \mathcal{Q}\}$$

respectively.

The *difference* obtained by subtracting the set B from the set A, denoted by $A - B$, is the set (shaded in Fig. 3.4) defined by

$$A - B = \{x : x \in A \quad \text{and} \quad x \notin B\}.$$

Notice that the operation of subtraction can be performed with any two sets. It is not required that B should be somehow "smaller" than A in order to form the set $A - B$.

The *complement* of a set A, denoted by A', is the set (shaded in Fig. 3.5) defined by

$$A' = \{x : x \notin A\}.$$

Notice that, no matter what set A is chosen, the sets A and A' are always disjoint.

Example 3.1 Let the universal set be $X = \{1, 2, \ldots, 10\}$, and set $A = \{2, 5, 7, 8\}$, $B = \{1, 5, 8, 10\}$, $C = \{3, 6, 9\}$. Then it is easy to check each of the following statements.

$A \cup B = \{1, 2, 5, 7, 8, 10\}$. (Notice that each of the objects 5 and 8, which are elements of A and also of B, appears only once as an element of $A \cup B$.)

$A \cap B = \{5, 8\}$.

$A \cap C = \emptyset$, so that A and C are disjoint.

$A - B = \{2, 7\}$.

$A - C = \{2, 5, 7, 8\} = A$.

$A' \cup B' = \{1, 2, 3, 4, 6, 7, 9, 10\} = (A \cap B)'$.

$A' \cap B' = \{3, 4, 6, 9\} = (A \cup B)'$.

$\qquad C \subset A' \cap B'$.

FIGURE 3.4   FIGURE 3.5

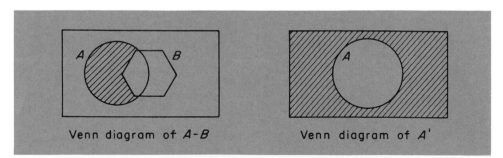

Venn diagram of *A-B*   Venn diagram of *A'*

For any sets A and B, the difference $A - B$ can be expressed in terms of the other operations. It is easy to see from Fig. 3.4 that $A - B = A \cap B'$. The most important properties of the operations of union, intersection, and complement are given in Theorem 3.1. Other properties, as well as those of subtraction, are dealt with in the problems.

Theorem 3.1 The operations of union, intersection, and complement satisfy the conditions listed below. Here X is the universal set, A, B, and C are any subsets of X, and $\emptyset$ is the empty set.

Commutative Laws:
$$A \cup B = B \cup A. \qquad A \cap B = B \cap A.$$

Associative Laws:
$$(A \cup B) \cup C = A \cup (B \cup C). \qquad (A \cap B) \cap C = A \cap (B \cap C).$$

Idempotent Laws:
$$A \cup A = A. \qquad A \cap A = A.$$

Distributive Laws:
$$A \cap (B \cup C) = (A \cap B) \cup (A \cap C).$$
$$A \cup (B \cap C) = (A \cup B) \cap (A \cup C).$$

DeMorgan's Laws:
$$(A \cup B)' = A' \cap B'. \qquad (A \cap B)' = A' \cup B'.$$

Laws of Complementation:
$$(A')' = A. \qquad A \cap A' = \emptyset. \qquad A \cup A' = X.$$

Special Properties of $\emptyset$ and $\mathbf{X}$:
$$A \cup \emptyset = A. \qquad A \cup X = X. \qquad \emptyset' = X.$$
$$A \cap \emptyset = \emptyset. \qquad A \cap X = A. \qquad X' = \emptyset.$$

REMARK. Because of the associative laws, we shall write expressions such as $A \cup B \cup C$ with no parentheses, since the result of performing the operations does not depend on the way in which the parentheses are inserted.

PROOF. To illustrate the methods used, we shall prove the first of the two distributive laws and the first of DeMorgan's laws; the proofs of the other parts of the theorem are left as exercises (Problem 3).

Proof of $A \cap (B \cup C) = (A \cap B) \cup (A \cap C)$. From Problem 5 of Section 6-2, this equation is equivalent to the two inclusions

$$A \cap (B \cup C) \subset (A \cap B) \cup (A \cap C)$$

and
$$A \cap (B \cup C) \supset (A \cap B) \cup (A \cap C).$$

The first of these inclusions can be proved by noticing that if x is any element of $A \cap (B \cup C)$, then $x \in A$ and $x \in B \cup C$. That is, x is an element of A, and x is an element of at least one of the sets B and C. But this means that x is an element of both A and B, or that x is an element of both A and C; hence,

$$x \in (A \cap B) \cup (A \cap C).$$

The second inclusion above can be proved by reversing the steps in the proof of the first inclusion. If

$$x \in (A \cap B) \cup (A \cap C),$$

then $x \in A \cap B$ or $x \in A \cap C$. In either case $x \in A$, and x is an element of at least one of the sets B and C; thus $x \in A$ and $x \in B \cup C$. It follows that

$$x \in A \cap (B \cup C).$$

Proof of $(A \cup B)' = A' \cap B'$. Again, we replace this equation by two inclusions and shall prove that

$$(A \cup B)' \subset A' \cap B' \quad \text{and} \quad (A \cup B)' \supset A' \cap B'.,$$

If $x \in (A \cup B)'$, then $x \notin A \cup B$. This means that x is not an element of either one of the sets A and B; hence $x \in A'$ and $x \in B'$, which gives $x \in A' \cap B'$. The other inclusion can be proved by reversing these steps«.

PROBLEMS

1. Define sets N, E, O, T, P as follows:

$N = \{1, 2, 3, \ldots\}$. (Take N as the universal set.)

$E = \{2, 4, 6, \ldots\}$, $O = \{1, 3, 5, \ldots\}$,

$T = \{3, 6, 9, \ldots\}$, $P = \{2, 3, 5, 7, 11, \ldots\}$. ($P$ is the set of all prime numbers.) Find a simple description, and list some of the elements of each of the following sets.

    (a) $E \cup O$.   (e) $T \cap (E \cup P)$.

    (b) $E \cap O$.   (f) $(T \cap E) \cup (T \cap P)$.

    (c) $E \cup T'$.   (g) $(P \cap O') \cup (P' \cap O)$.

    (d) $(E \cup T)'$.   (h) $\{[(E \cap O') \cup (E' \cap O)]' \cup P\}'$.

2. Give a representation, using Venn diagrams, of the distributive law and DeMorgan's law (Theorem 3.1) which were proved in the text.

3. **(a)** Prove the second distributive law and represent the result by a Venn diagram.
(b) Prove the parts of Theorem 3.1 which have not already been proved, and draw Venn diagrams illustrating the statements.

4. Prove that the following statements are all equivalent.

      (a) $A \subset B$.   **(d)** $A - B = \emptyset$.
      (b) $A \cap B = A$.   **(e)** $A' \supset B'$.
      (c) $A \cup B = B$.   **(f)** $A \cap B' = \emptyset$.

5. Prove that each of the following conditions is necessary and sufficient for the sets A and B to be disjoint.

      (a) $A - B = A$ **(c)** $A \subset B'$
      (b) $B - A = B$ **(d)** $A' \cup B' = X$

6. Is it possible for a set to be disjoint from one of its subsets? Can a set be disjoint from itself?

7. Simplify each of the following.

    (a) $\{[(A \cup B) \cap (A \cup A')] \cup B'\}'$.
    (b) $\{[(A' \cap B)' \cup (A' \cap A)] \cap B\}'$.
    (c) $\{[(A \cup B') \cap A'] \cup B'\}$.
    (d) $\{[(A \cup B)' \cap A]' \cup B\}'$.

8. Prove that for any sets A, B, C, each of the following equations is correct. Illustrate the results with Venn diagrams.

    (a) $(A - B) - C = A - (B \cup C) = (A - B) \cap (A - C)$.
    (b) $A - (B - C) = (A - B) \cup (A \cap B \cap C)$.
    (c) $A - (B \cap C) = (A - B) \cup (A - C)$.
    (d) $A \cap (B - C) = (A \cap B) - (A \cap C)$.
    (e) $A \cup (B - C) = (A \cup B) - [(B \cap C) - A]$.
    (f) $(A - B)' = A' \cup B$.

9. For any sets A and B, define

$$A \triangle B = (A \cup B) - (A \cap B).$$

(a) Prove that $A \triangle B = (A - B) \cup (B - A)$.
(b) Find a set Z such that, for each set A, $A \triangle Z = A$, and show that there is only one set Z satisfying these conditions.
(c) For each set A, find a set A^* such that $A \triangle A^* = Z$, and prove that, for each A, the set A^* is unique.
(d) Prove that $(A \triangle B) \triangle C = A \triangle (B \triangle C)$.
(e) Prove that A and B are disjoint if and only if $A \triangle B = A \cup B$.

10. Compare the operations of union, intersection, and subtraction of sets with the operations addition, multiplication, and subtraction of numbers, resspectively. In what ways are the two sets of operations similar? In what ways do they differ?

11. Let B be any given set and define

$$\mathcal{C} = \{A : A \subset B\}.$$

(a) What is $\cup \{A : A \in \mathcal{C}\}$?
(b) What is $\cap \{A : A \in \mathcal{C}\}$?

12. In Section 6-2 we noticed that a study of the relations of equality and inclusion between sets could be considered as a study of the relations of equivalence and implication between sentential functions. What aspects of sentential functions correspond to the operations $\cup$, $\cap$, $-$, and $'$ for sets? [Hint: Suppose $A = \{x : S(x)\}$ and $B = \{x : T(x)\}$ and find descriptions of the sets $A \cup B$, $A \cap B$, etc.]

13. Simplify each of the following.
(a) $[A' \cap (B \cup C)]'$.
(b) $[(A \cup B) \cup C']'$.
(c) $[(A \cup B) \cap (B \cup C) \cap (A \cup C)]'$.
(d) $A - [B - (C \cup D)]$.
(e) $A - [B - (C - D)]$.
(f) $A - [B - (C \cap D)]$.
(g) $A \cap [(A \cup B) - B]$.
(h) $(A - B) \cap [(A \cap B) \cup (A - C)]$.
(i) $(A \cap C') \cup (A \cap B \cap C) \cup (A \cap C)$.
(j) $(A \cap B \cap C) \cup A' \cup B' \cup C'$.
(k) $[A \cup (A \cap B) \cup (A \cap B \cap C)] \cap [A \cup B \cup C]$.
(l) $[(P \cap Q) \cup (P' \cap Q') \cup (P \cap Q')]' \cap [(P' \cup Q') \cap (P \cup Q')]'$.
(m) $[(P \cap Q) \cup (A \cap B \cap C)] \cap [(P \cap Q) \cup A' \cup B' \cup C']$.

Transformations

7–1 Introduction

In Chapter 1 we used the concept of an elastic
motion to give a tentative definition of topology;
in Chapter 3 we remarked that a real understanding of the concept of an elastic motion would
require some knowledge of set theory, which we
have gained in Chapter 6. In this chapter we
shall be able to explain more clearly just what
we have had in mind in connection with this
concept. Unfortunately, the term "elastic motion" carries with it some undesirable intuitive
connotations. Chief among these undesirable
connotations is the idea that "motion" from one

place to another necessarily entails some sort of path, or route, along which this motion takes place. In Section 7-2 we define a transformation — the thing we have really meant all the time by "motion" — and it will be evident that no path, or route, is needed for a transformation. The discussion in Section 7-2 is applicable to arbitrary sets. In Section 7-3 we confine our attention to subsets of ordinary three-dimensional Euclidean space. For these sets, we shall define a homeomorphism, or topological transformation, and shall point out that this new concept is what we have been attempting to suggest all along by the intuitive idea of an elastic motion. Two indices of transformations are discussed in Section 7-4 and, in Section 7-5, these indices are used to prove Brouwer's fixed point theorem and the fundamental theorem of algebra.

7–2 Transformations Between Arbitrary Sets

Let X and Y be any sets; by a *transformation from X into Y* we mean a correspondence which determines, for each element $x \in X$, exactly one element $y \in Y$. That is, there must be a rule, or procedure, such that whenever a particular element $x_0 \in X$ is chosen, the rule determines exactly one element $y_0 \in Y$. We say that the element y_0 determined in this way corresponds to x_0 under the transformation (or that y_0 is the image of x_0, or that x_0 is sent into y_0, etc.).

It is important to notice certain things which are not required in the definition of a transformation. For instance, if x_1 and x_2 are two different elements of X, their corresponding elements y_1 and y_2 in Y may be different, or they may be the same element; the definition makes no requirement on this point. Also, for certain of the elements $y \in Y$, there may be no elements in X to which they correspond. All that is required is that, for each $x \in X$, there is exactly one corresponding $y \in Y$. We use a notation such as f, or $f : X \to Y$ (other letters may be used instead of f), for a transformation from X into Y and, for each $x \in X$, we denote by $f(x)$ the element of Y which is the image of x under the transformation. If every element $y \in Y$ is the image of at least one element $x \in X$, we say that the transformation is from X *onto* Y.

One way of defining a transformation is to give a rule which can be used to determine the image of an arbitrary element $x \in X$; that is, to give a procedure for determining an element $f(x) \in Y$ for each element $x \in X$. This method is used to define the transformations in the following examples. These examples are continued later in this section.

Example 2.1 Each of the sets X and Y is the set of all real numbers; $f(x) = 2x$. The transformation $f : X \rightarrow Y$ is onto Y.

Example 2.2 Each of X and Y is the set of all real numbers; $g(x) = x^2$. The transformation $g : X \rightarrow Y$ is into Y, but not onto Y.

Example 2.3 X is the set of all real numbers; $Y = \{0, 1\}$.

$$h(x) = \begin{cases} 0, & \text{if } x \text{ is rational.} \\ 1, & \text{if } x \text{ is irrational.} \end{cases}$$

The transformation $h : X \rightarrow Y$ is onto Y.

Example 2.4 X is an arbitrary set and $Y = X$; $i(x) = x$. The transformation $i : X \rightarrow X$ is called the *identity* transformation on X; it is onto X.

It is evident from the definition of a transformation, and from the examples given above, that there is no physical motion, or movement, occasioned by a transformation. The element $x \in X$ does not "move" to the element $f(x) \in Y$; x is merely made to correspond to $f(x)$. The elements x and $f(x)$ can be thought of as being associated in some way, with the particular association being described by the transformation f; however, this association cannot usually be pictured as a physical motion.

The correspondence given by the transformation $f : X \rightarrow Y$ is from an element $x \in X$ to an element $y = f(x) \in Y$. It is frequently convenient to consider the correspondence obtained by reversing the given one. For each element $y \in Y$ we define the *inverse image* of y under f, denoted by $f^{-1}(y)$, to be the set of all elements of X which correspond to y. That is,

$$f^{-1}(y) = \{x : x \in X \quad \text{and} \quad f(x) = y\}.$$

For any subset $B \subset Y$, the inverse image of B under f, denoted by $f^{-1}(B)$, is the set of all elements $x \in X$ whose images are in B; that is,

$$f^{-1}(B) = \{x : x \in X \quad \text{and} \quad f(x) \in B\}.$$

Similarly, for any set $A \subset X$, we define

$$f(A) = \{y : y \text{ corresponds to some element } x \in A\}.$$

It may happen that, for certain elements $y \in Y$, $f^{-1}(y)$ is the empty set, or $f^{-1}(y)$ may be a set having a great many elements. If, for each element $y \in Y$, the set $f^{-1}(y)$ is a singleton (that is, if each $y \in Y$ corresponds to exactly one element $x \in X$), we say that the transformation f is *one-to-one* and we write $f^{-1}(y) = x$ instead of $f^{-1}(y) = \{x\}$. In this case, the correspondence $f^{-1} : Y \rightarrow X$ is a transformation which is called the *inverse* of the transformation $f: X \rightarrow Y$. Notice that, for every transformation $f: X \rightarrow Y$, we have defined a correspondence f^{-1} from subsets of Y to subsets of X, but in order that this correspondence be called the inverse transformation of f, it is required that f be one-to-one.

There are several interesting and important results concerned with one-to-one transformations. If there is a one-to-one transformation of X onto Y, it is natural to say that the sets X and Y have the same number of elements. However, if $N = \{1, 2, 3, \ldots\}$ is the set of all positive integers and $E = \{2, 4, 6, \ldots\}$ is the set of all positive even integers, then the transformation given by $f(n) = 2n$ for each $n \in N$, is a one-to-one transformation of N onto its proper subset E. It seems paradoxical that a proper subset of N could have the same number of elements as N, but, on the other hand, if the set N is in one-to-one correspondence with the set E, surely there cannot be more elements in one set than in the other.

The concept of "same number of elements," based on the existence of a one-to-one transformation, has been found to be a fruitful one. Formally, the definition states that two sets A and B have the same *cardinal number* if and only if there is a one-to-one transformation from A onto B. With this definition, the statement "the whole is greater than any one of its parts" which is customarily given as one of the postulates, or "common notions" of Euclid, is actually not correct. Some further results are suggested in the problems.

Example 2.1 (continued) The inverse of the transformation $f : X \rightarrow Y$ is the transformation $f^{-1} : Y \rightarrow X$ given by $f^{-1}(y) = \frac{1}{2}y$.

Example 2.2 (continued) The transformation $g : X \rightarrow Y$ does not have an inverse transformation, since $g^{-1}(-2) = \emptyset$; also $g^{-1}(1) = \{1, -1\}$, which is not a singleton.

Example 2.3 (continued) The transformation $h : X \rightarrow Y$ does not have an inverse transformation, since $h^{-1}(0)$ is a set with an infinite number of elements.

Example 2.4 (continued) The transformation $i : X \rightarrow X$ is its own inverse.

PROBLEMS

1. Discuss each of the following. In which cases is $f: X \rightarrow Y$ a transformation?   In which cases is f onto Y?   In which is it one-to-one?   Which transformations have an inverse?

(a) Each of X and Y is the set of all real numbers.

$$f(x) = \begin{cases} 1/x, & \text{if } x < 0. \\ 2, & \text{if } x = 0. \\ x^2, & \text{if } x > 0. \end{cases}$$

(b) X is the collection of all people residing in the United States; Y is the set whose elements are the 50 states; $f(x)$ is the state in which x resides.

(c) Let $f(x)$ be the area of x.   (What sets are you using for X and Y?)

(d) Each of X and Y is the set of all real numbers.

$$f(x) = \begin{cases} 0, & \text{if } x \text{ is irrational.} \\ 1/q, & \text{if } x \text{ is rational and equals } p/q, \\ & \text{where } p \text{ and } q \text{ are integers.} \end{cases}$$

(e) Define $f(x)$ to be a grandchild of x.   (What are the sets X and Y?)

(f) X is the set of chairs in a particular classroom in which a class is meeting; Y is the set of all students registered for that class; $f(x)$ is the student sitting in x.   (Are some other sets more suitable than X and Y for discussing this situation?   What if some student is absent, or reciting at the board?   What if some visitors are seated in the classroom?)

2. Set $A = \{x: -1 \leq x \leq 1\}$ and $B = \{0, 1\}$.   With the functions f, g, and h of Examples 2.1 to 2.3, find

(a) $f(A)$ (e) $g(B)$ (i) $f^{-1}(B)$
(b) $g(A)$ (f) $h(B)$ (j) $g^{-1}(B)$
(c) $h(A)$ (g) $f^{-1}(A)$ (k) $h^{-1}(B)$
(d) $f(B)$ (h) $g^{-1}(A)$

3. Let $f: X \rightarrow Y$ be a transformation, and let A and B be any subsets of X.
(a) Show that $f(A \cup B) = f(A) \cup f(B)$.
(b) Show that $f(A \cap B) \subset f(A) \cap f(B)$, and give an example to show that the inclusion sign cannot always be replaced by an equality.
(c) Show that $f^{-1}(f(A)) \supset A$, and give an example to show that the inclusion sign cannot always be replaced by an equality.

4. Let $f: X \rightarrow Y$ be a transformation and let A and B be any subsets of Y.
(a) Show that $f^{-1}(A \cup B) = f^{-1}(A) \cup f^{-1}(B)$.
(b) Show that $f^{-1}(A \cap B) = f^{-1}(A) \cap f^{-1}(B)$.
(c) Show that $f^{-1}(A') = [f^{-1}(A)]'$.
(d) Show that $f^{-1}(A - B) = f^{-1}(A) - f^{-1}(B)$.
(e) Show that $f(f^{-1}(A)) \subset A$, and give an example to show that the inclusion sign cannot always be replaced by an equality.

5. (**a**) If $X = \{1, 2, 3\}$ and $Y = \{1, 2\}$, how many different transformations $f: X \to Y$ are there?
(**b**) If $X = \{1, 2, \ldots, n\}$ and $Y = \{1, 2, \ldots, m\}$, how many different transformations $f: X \to Y$ are there?

6. Let $f: X \to Y$ be the transformation of Example 2.1.
(**a**) For what real numbers x is it true that $f(x) = x$?
(**b**) For what sets A is it true that $f(A) = A$?
(**c**) Answer the questions in parts (a) and (b) if the transformation $g: X \to Y$ of Example 2.2 is used instead of f.

7. (**a**) Show that there is a one-to-one transformation from the set $N = \{1, 2, 3, \ldots\}$ onto the set F of all positive rational numbers. (A positive rational number is the quotient of two positive integers.)
*(**b**) Show that there is no one-to-one transformation from the set N onto the set $I = \{x : 0 \leq x \leq 1\}$. (Hint: Express each $x \in I$ as an infinite decimal and assume there is a one-to-one transformation $f: N \to I$. Form an infinite decimal d such that, for each $n \in N$, the nth decimal place of d is different from the nth decimal place of $f(n)$. Show that $d \in I$, but $d \notin f(N)$; this is a contradiction.)

8. Let X, Y, and Z be any sets.
(**a**) Show that X has the same cardinal number as X.
(**b**) Show that if X and Y have the same cardinal number, then Y and X have the same cardinal number.
(**c**) Show that if X and Y have the same cardinal number, and Y and Z have the same cardinal number, then X and Z have the same cardinal number.

7–3 Transformations Between Subsets of Three-Dimensional Euclidean Space

A transformation $f: X \to Y$ becomes more interesting if there is some "structure" in the sets X and Y; that is, if there are some properties of the elements, or of sets of elements, in which we are interested. We can then inquire whether these properties are preserved by the transformation or by its inverse. With this idea in mind, we shall confine our discussion in this section to transformations in which both of the sets X and Y are subsets of three-dimensional Euclidean space. Because of its geometric interpretation, we shall speak of "points" instead of "elements" of X and Y. The "structure" with which we shall endow these sets stems from the concept of the distance between two points. For any points p and q

of three-dimensional space, we shall denote the distance from p to q by $d(p, q)$; we recall that this distance satisfies the following conditions:

For any points p, q, r,

(1) $d(p, q) \geq 0$. (Therefore, $d(p, q)$ is a real number.)
(2) $d(p, q) = 0$ iff $p = q$.
(3) $d(p, q) = d(q, p)$.
(4) $d(p, q) + d(q, r) \geq d(p, r)$.

The first condition states that for any two points (or for the same point taken twice), there is a distance from one point to the other, and this distance is a non-negative real number. Condition 2 contains two bits of information. It says that the distance from any point to itself is zero, and also that the distance from any point to a different point is never zero. Condition 3 tells us that the distance from one point to another is always the same as the distance from the second point back to the first. Because of this symmetry relation, we can speak of the distance between two points, instead of the distance from one point to another. The fourth condition is called the triangle inequality; the points p, q, and r can be thought of as the vertices of a triangle (the triangle may degenerate into a line segment), and, with this interpretation, the condition states that the sum of the lengths of any two sides of a triangle is at least as big as the length of the third side.

Thus each of these four conditions states a very simple fact about distances in three-dimensional Euclidean space. It would be possible to mention many other properties of distances, but these four conditions will play an especially important role in the work of the next chapter.

In Section 7-2 we saw several examples of transformations between sets in which the elements were objects of various types. To gain familiarity with the special case of transformations between subsets of three-dimensional space, several examples of transformations of this type are given below.

Example 3.1 Let each of the sets X and Y be the real numbers; then X and Y can be represented by two lines (or by the same line) in three-dimensional space. Thus any transformation $f : X \rightarrow Y$, where X and Y are each the set of real numbers, can be thought of as a transformation between subsets of three-dimensional space. In the future, whenever it is convenient, we shall identify the real numbers with any particular line in three-dimensional space, and shall call a line an X-axis iff X is the set of real numbers and the line is identified with X; similarly, for a Y-axis.

Example 3.2 Let X and Y be the same plane in three-dimensional space. A transformation $f : X \rightarrow Y$ is given by any physical motion of the plane (for example, a translation or rotation) which is such that each point of the plane is carried by the motion into a point in that same plane. The rule of correspondence is that, for any point $x \in X$, $f(x)$ is the point of the plane into which the point x is carried by the motion. As special cases of such motions, we may consider the following.

   (a) Translation. Each point $x \in X$ can be assigned Cartesian coordinates (x_1, x_2); then $f(x)$ is the point whose coordinates are $(x_1 + h, x_2 + k)$, where h and k are two given constants.

   (b) Rotation. For each point $x = (x_1, x_2)$ of the plane, the corresponding point is

$$f(x) = (x_1 \cos \theta - x_2 \sin \theta, \ x_1 \sin \theta + x_2 \cos \theta)$$

where θ is a given constant. Of course, the points in the plane could be represented by polar coordinates instead of rectangular coordinates. The transformation is a correspondence between the points themselves, and this correspondence can be described in several different ways.

   (c) A stretching (or shrinking) of the plane. For any point $x = (x_1, x_2) \in X$, set $f(x) = (hx_1, kx_2)$, where h and k are given constants. In this example, if $h = k$, the plane is stretched away from the origin if $h > 1$, and is shrunk toward the origin if $h < 1$; if $h = k = 1$ we obtain the identity transformation on the plane. Notice that the identity transformation is an example of each of the three types: translation, rotation, and stretching. If $h \neq k$, the physical movement is a little harder to picture, but consists of two different stretchings (or shrinkings) which operate in different directions.

FIGURE 3.1

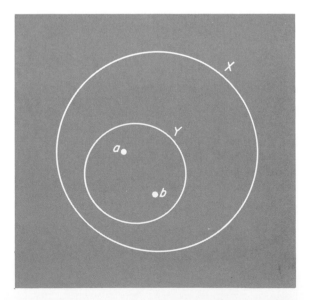

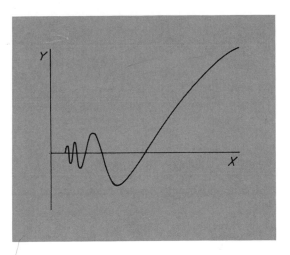

FIGURE 3.2

Example 3.3 Let X be a closed ball, and let Y be a closed ball included in X (Fig. 3.1); for each $x \in X$, define $f(x)$ to be the point of Y which is closest to x.

Let a and b be two distinct points of Y; two more transformations $g : X \to Y$ and $h : X \to Y$ can be defined as follows:

For each $x \in X$, set $g(x) = a$.

For each $x \in X$, set

$$h(x) = \begin{cases} a, & \text{if } x \in Y. \\ b, & \text{if } x \notin Y. \end{cases}$$

Example 3.4 X is the X-axis and Y is the origin together with the graph of the equation $y = x \sin (1/x)$ (in a plane, *see* Fig. 3.2). For each point $x \in X$, let $f(x)$ be the point (x, y) of Y whose first coordinate is the real number x. (Notice that we have identified the real numbers with the X-axis.)

We are now ready to use the concept of distance in three-dimensional space to define continuity of transformations. A transformation $f : X \to Y$ is *continuous at the point* $x_0 \in X$ iff, given any real number $\varepsilon > 0$, there is a real number $\delta > 0$ such that:

If $x \in X$ and $d(x_0, x) < \delta$, then $d(f(x_0), f(x)) < \varepsilon$.

A transformation $f : X \to Y$ is *continuous* iff it is continuous at each point of X.

Continuity, and some related concepts which we shall meet later, are of fundamental importance in all of mathematical analysis. It is, therefore, extremely important not only that each mathematics student should know the definition of a continuous transformation, but that he should also have an understanding of what the definition says. Very roughly (and inaccurately), the transformation $f: X \to Y$ is continuous at the point $x_0 \in X$ iff, whenever a point $x \in X$ is near to x_0, its image $f(x)$ is near to the image $f(x_0)$ of x_0. The inaccuracy in this form of the statement arises from not knowing just what is meant by "near." In fact, in the statement of the definition, it can be seen that there are two different standards of "nearness" which are used. For any positive real number r, let us call the two points p and q of three-dimensional space r-near iff $d(p, q) < r$. It is evident, from the definition of continuity at x_0, that we are using δ-nearness in the set X and ε-nearness in the set Y. With this notation, the definition says that a positive value for ε can be chosen arbitrarily and that, after this choice has been made, it must be possible to find a $\delta > 0$ such that:

> If $x \in X$ and x is δ-near to x_0, then $f(x)$ is ε-near to $f(x_0)$.

Thus the standard of nearness in Y is chosen first, and, for every such choice, there must be a standard of nearness in X so that these two standards of nearness are related as required by the definition.

Notice that x_0 represents one and the same point throughout the discussion in the preceding paragraph. That is, all of this discussion is concerned with a property having something to do with the particular point x_0. The property, of course, is continuity of f at x_0. (From our definition it is meaningless to discuss continuity of f at points $z \notin X$.) For the related property, continuity of the transformation f, it is required that f should be continuous at each point $x_0 \in X$. That is, for each choice of a point $x_0 \in X$ and a number $\varepsilon > 0$, there must be a $\delta > 0$ which satisfies the appropriate condition. Notice that the value of δ may depend on both x_0 and ε, since both of these are chosen before δ is found.

Example 3.5 Let $X = Y = \{x : x > 0\}$, and set $f(x) = 1/x$. Then $f : X \to Y$ is a one-to-one transformation from X onto Y. We shall give two proofs that the transformation f is continuous. The first proof is analytic in nature, and is in the form in which such proofs are frequently presented; the second proof is more intuitive, and indicates how the first proof could be discovered.

First Proof. Given any point $x_0 \in X$, and any $\varepsilon > 0$, choose

$$\delta = \frac{\varepsilon x_0^2}{1 + \varepsilon x_0}.$$

Now suppose that $x \in X$ is δ-near to x_0, i.e., that $d(x_0, x) < \delta$; we must show that $f(x)$ is ϵ-near to $f(x_0)$. We find

$$d(f(x_0), f(x)) = \left| \frac{1}{x_0} - \frac{1}{x} \right| = \frac{|x - x_0|}{xx_0} = \frac{d(x_0, x)}{x_0 x} < \frac{\delta}{x_0 x} .$$

But, since

$$\delta = \frac{\epsilon x_0^2}{1 + \epsilon x_0} ,$$

and x is δ-near to x_0,

$$x_0 x \geq x_0(x_0 - \delta) = x_0 \left(x_0 - \frac{\epsilon x_0^2}{1 + \epsilon x_0} \right)$$

and

$$d(f(x_0), f(x)) < \frac{\delta}{x_0 x} \leq \frac{\dfrac{\epsilon x_0^2}{1 + \epsilon x_0}}{x_0 \left(x_0 - \dfrac{\epsilon x_0^2}{1 + \epsilon x_0} \right)}$$

$$= \frac{\epsilon x_0^2}{x_0^2(1 + \epsilon x_0 - \epsilon x_0)} - \epsilon.$$

SECOND PROOF. Figure 3.3 shows the sets X and Y represented as portions of lines in three-dimensional space. Given any point $x_0 \in X$, and any $\epsilon > 0$, we first locate the point $f(x_0) = 1/x_0 \in Y$, and then locate the subset of Y composed of all the points of Y which are ϵ-near to $f(x_0)$. This subset is the heavy

FIGURE 3.3

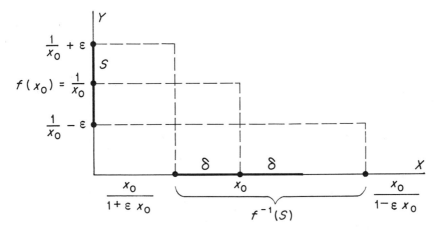

vertical segment S in Fig. 3.3. Next we find the subset $f^{-1}(S)$, composed of all points of X which correspond to points of S. The set $f^{-1}(S)$ is a segment with x_0 to the left of its center. Now we must find a positive number δ such that if x is δ-near to x_0, then $x \in f^{-1}(S)$. Clearly, we may take δ as the distance from x_0 to the left (nearest) end point of the segment $f^{-1}(S)$. Thus we choose

$$\delta = x_0 - \frac{1}{\dfrac{1}{x_0} + \varepsilon} = x_0 - \frac{x_0}{1 + \varepsilon x_0} = \frac{\varepsilon x_0^2}{1 + \varepsilon x_0}.$$

There is another remark that should be made. Figure 3.3 is somewhat misleading in certain cases. If $\varepsilon x_0 \geq 1$, then the point shown as the lower end of the interval S is not in Y (since its coordinate is not positive). In all cases, the set S is chosen as the subset of Y composed of the points of Y which are ε-near to $f(x_0)$. The upper end point of S, and not the lower one, was used to determine δ; thus the possibility that the lower end point indicated in Fig. 3.3 may actually be incorrect has no effect on the choice of δ, and our result is correct in all cases.

Example 3.6 Let each of X and Y be the set of all real numbers and define

$$f(x) = \begin{cases} 0, & \text{if } x \leq 0. \\ 1, & \text{if } x > 0. \end{cases}$$

Then if x_0 is any point of X except 0, it can be proved by an argument similar to the one in Example 3.5 above that $f : X \to Y$ is continuous at x_0. Let us consider the special choices $x_0 = 0$, $\varepsilon = \frac{1}{2}$. Then no matter what positive value is taken for δ, the point $x_1 = \frac{1}{2}\delta$ will be δ-near to x_0. But the image of this point is $f(x_1) = 1$, and this image is not $\frac{1}{2}$-near to $f(x_0) = 0$. Thus $f : X \to Y$ is not continuous at the point 0.

Example 3.7 Let each of X and Y be the set of points with positive integral coordinates along a line; that is,

$$X = Y = \{1, 2, 3, \ldots\}.$$

Define a transformation $f : X \to Y$ by setting $f(x) = 2x$. Then f is a continuous transformation of X into Y (but not onto Y). In fact, for any $x_0 \in X$ and any $\varepsilon > 0$, we may choose $\delta = \frac{1}{2}$, since, if $x \in X$ and x is $\frac{1}{2}$-near to x_0, then $x = x_0$ and it follows that $f(x) = f(x_0)$, so $f(x)$ is ε-near to $f(x_0)$ no matter what positive value of ε was chosen.

We are now in a position to sharpen our understanding of the type of problems that are considered in topology. A *homeomorphism* or *topological transformation* is a transformation which is continuous and which has a continuous inverse transformation. The concept of a homeomorphism is what we have tried to suggest in the past by the term "elastic motion." Two subsets X and Y of three-dimensional space are *homeomorphic* or *topologically equivalent* iff there is a homeomorphism $f: X \rightarrow Y$. The transformations in Examples 3.2a, 3.2b, 3.2c (if $h \neq 0$ and $k \neq 0$), 3.4, and 3.5 are homeomorphisms. Other examples and properties are presented in the problems. Topology is the study of properties which are invariant under homeomorphisms.

In some important special cases, there are ways of combining two transformations to obtain a third one. That is, there are binary operations on transformations. We shall confine our attention here to the case where $X = Y$ and each of these sets is the set of all real numbers, and we shall represent these sets by a line, as usual. We define three binary operations as follows:

If $f: X \rightarrow X$ and $g: X \rightarrow X$ are any two transformations,

$f+g: X \rightarrow X$ is defined by setting $(f+g)(x) = f(x) + g(x)$;

$fg: X \rightarrow X$ is defined by setting $(fg)(x) = f(x)g(x)$;

$f \bigcirc g: X \rightarrow X$ is defined by setting $(f \bigcirc g)(x) = f(g(x))$.

These three operations are called addition, multiplication, and composition, respectively. We shall also consider multiplication of a transformation by a real number r. This operation is defined by the equation

$$(rf)(x) = rf(x).$$

As an example, if $f(x) = x^2$, and $g(x) = x^3$, then $(f+g)(x) = x^2 + x^3$, $(fg)(x) = x^5$, $(f \bigcirc g)(x) = x^6$, $(7f)(x) = 7x^2$.

Theorem 3.1 If X is the set of real numbers and each of $f: X \rightarrow X$ and $g: X \rightarrow X$ is a continuous transformation, then each of the transformations $f+g, fg,$ and $f \bigcirc g$ is continuous; also, for any real number r, the transformation rf is continuous.

PROOF. We give the proof for the function $f+g$; the other cases are left as exercises (Problem 2). If $x_0 \in X$ and $\varepsilon > 0$ are given, choose $\delta_1 > 0$ and $\delta_2 > 0$ so that

If x is δ_1-near to x_0, then $f(x)$ is $\dfrac{\varepsilon}{2}$-near to $f(x_0)$,

and

If x is δ_2-near to x_0, then $g(x)$ is $\dfrac{\varepsilon}{2}$-near to $g(x_0)$.

The choices of δ_1 and δ_2 are possible because f and g are continuous. Now choose δ as the smaller of δ_1 and δ_2, and we find that if x is δ-near to x_0, then $f(x)$ is $\frac{\varepsilon}{2}$-near to $f(x_0)$ and also $g(x)$ is $\frac{\varepsilon}{2}$-near to $g(x_0)$. This means that

$$|f(x) - f(x_0)| < \frac{\varepsilon}{2} \quad \text{and} \quad |g(x) - g(x_0)| < \frac{\varepsilon}{2}.$$

But then

$$|(f+g)(x) - (f+g)(x_0)| = |f(x) + g(x) - f(x_0) - g(x_0)|$$
$$\leq |f(x) - f(x_0)| + |g(x) - g(x_0)| < \varepsilon.$$

Since $(f+g)(x)$ is ε-near to $(f+g)(x_0)$, $f+g$ is continuous at x_0. Since x_0 was an arbitrary point, the function $f+g$ is continuous «.

For any real polynomial $a_0x^n + a_1x^{n-1} + \cdots + a_n$, we may define a transformation $f: X \rightarrow X$ of the real numbers into themselves by setting

$$f(x) = a_0x^n + a_1x^{n-1} + \cdots + a_n.$$

It is an easy consequence of Theorem 3.1 that this transformation is continuous.

PROBLEMS

1. Discuss each of the following transformations with reference to the questions: At which points is the transformation continuous? Is there an inverse transformation? At which points is the inverse transformation continuous? Is the transformation a homeomorphism?
(a) The transformation $g: X \rightarrow Y$ defined in Example 3.3.
(b) The transformation $h: X \rightarrow Y$ defined in Example 3.3. (Hint: Consider various cases according as the points a and b are, or are not, on the boundary sphere of the ball Y.)
(c) The transformation $f: X \rightarrow Y$ defined in Example 3.3.
(d) A translation of a plane (Example 3.2a).
(e) A rotation of a plane (Example 3.2b).
(f) A stretching of a plane (Example 3.2c).
(g) The transformation $f: X \rightarrow Y$ defined in Example 3.4.
(h) Each of X and Y is the set of real numbers; the transformation $f: X \rightarrow Y$ is defined by

$$f(x) = \begin{cases} 1/x, & \text{if } x < 0. \\ 2, & \text{if } x = 0. \\ x^2, & \text{if } x > 0. \end{cases}$$

(i) Each of X and Y is the set of real numbers; the transformation $f: X \rightarrow Y$ is defined by

$$f(x) = \begin{cases} 0, & \text{if } x \text{ is irrational.} \\ 0, & \text{if } x = 0. \\ 1/q, & \text{if } x \text{ is rational, } \neq 0, \text{ and equals } p/q \\ & \text{when expressed in lowest terms} \\ & (q > 0, p \text{ and } q \text{ integers}). \end{cases}$$

(j) A closed disk is folded along a diameter. (What sets are you using for X and Y?)

(k) A closed ball is projected into a tangent plane. (What are X and Y?)

(l) A sphere is projected into a tangent plane.

2. (a) Let X be any subset of three-dimensional space. Prove that the identity transformation $i: X \rightarrow X$, defined by $i(x) = x$ for each $x \in X$, is a homeomorphism.

(b) Complete the proof of Theorem 3.1.

(c) Prove the statement made just before this set of problems, that any polynomial transformation is continuous.

(d) Let each of X and Y be the real numbers and let $f: X \rightarrow Y$ be a transformation. The student is already familiar with such transformations under the name "function." Show that in this special case, our definition of continuity is equivalent to the usual one found in calculus texts. We shall use this result in some other special cases (e.g., when X is the unit interval $I = \{x: 0 \leq x \leq 1\}$).

3. If $f: X \rightarrow Y$ and $g: Y \rightarrow Z$ are homeomorphisms, prove that $g \circ f$ is a homeomorphism from X onto Z.

4. For each point x in three-dimensional space, and for each positive real number r, let us denote the open ball with center x and radius r by $B(x; r)$. Prove that a transformation $f: X \rightarrow Y$ between subsets of three-dimensional space is continuous at $x_0 \in X$ if and only if, for each $\varepsilon > 0$, there is a $\delta > 0$ such that

$$X \cap B(x_0; \delta) \subset f^{-1}[Y \cap B(f(x_0); \varepsilon)]$$

#5. Let each of X and Y be all of three-dimensional space and use $B(x; r)$ as defined in Problem 4. Prove that $f: X \rightarrow Y$ is continuous if and only if, for each $y \in Y$ and each real number $r > 0$,

If $x \in f^{-1}(B(y; r))$, then there is an open ball $B(x; s)$

such that $B(x; s) \subset f^{-1}(B(y; r))$.

This condition can be rephrased: The inverse image of each open ball in Y contains some open ball about each of its points.

6. Let $f: X \to Y$ be a transformation between subsets of three-dimensional space, and let $\varepsilon > 0$ be a positive real number. Call a positive number δ "satisfactory at x_0" provided that

$$\text{If } x \in X \quad \text{and} \quad x \text{ is } \delta\text{-near to } x_0,$$

$$\text{then } f(x) \text{ is } \varepsilon\text{-near to } f(x_0).$$

(a) Prove that $f: X \to Y$ is continuous at x_0 iff, for each $\varepsilon > 0$, there is a $\delta > 0$ which is satisfactory at x_0.

(b) Prove that $f: X \to Y$ is continuous if and only if, for each point x_0 and each $\varepsilon > 0$, there is a $\delta > 0$ which is satisfactory at x_0.

(c) In Example 3.5, show that, for $\varepsilon = 1$, there is no value of δ which is satisfactory at all points $x \in X$. At which points is $\delta = \frac{1}{2}$ satisfactory?

7. Do Problem 4 of Section 1-2.

8. (a) Prove that the two subsets of three-dimensional space represented by the lines and curves in Fig. 3.4 are homeomorphic. (No surfaces are involved — only lines and curves.)

(b) In setting up a homeomorphism between the two figures of Fig. 3.4, which of the points s, t, u, v, w, x, y, z in Fig. 3.4b can correspond to each of the points a, b, c, d, e, f in Fig. 3.4a? (Caution: There are many different homeomorphisms between these two figures; the problem is to find which of the points $s, t, \ldots, z$ correspond to the point a under at least one of these homeomorphisms; similarly for b, c, d, e, f.)

9. Let X be the set of all real numbers, and let $f: X \to X$, $g: X \to X$, and $h: X \to X$ be transformations (not necessarily continuous). Prove that $(fg) \bigcirc h = (f \bigcirc h)(g \bigcirc h)$.

10. Let

$$X = \{(x_1, x_2): \ 0 \le x_1 \le 1 \quad \text{and} \quad 0 \le x_2 \le 1\}$$

be the unit square in a plane, and let

$$Y = \{y: 0 \le y \le 1\}$$

FIGURE 3.4

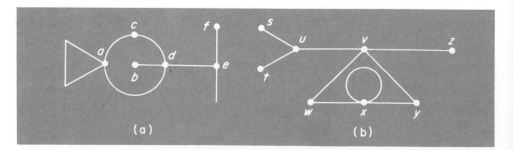

(a)   (b)

be a segment of length 1. Write each value of x_1 and x_2 as a decimal and, if two different decimal forms are available for a particular value, choose the form which has the digit 9 repeated. For example,

$$\tfrac{1}{2} = 0.5000 \ldots = 0.49999 \ldots ;$$

the form $0.49999 \ldots$ is chosen as the one to express the value of $\tfrac{1}{2}$. Define $f: X \to Y$ as follows: For each point $x = (x_1, x_2) \in X$, where

$$x_1 = 0.\xi_1 \xi_2 \xi_3 \ldots, \quad \text{and} \quad x_2 = 0.\eta_1 \eta_2 \eta_3 \ldots ,$$

set $f(x) = 0.\xi_1 \eta_1 \xi_2 \eta_2 \xi_3 \eta_3 \ldots .$ Is $f: X \to Y$ a transformation? Is it continuous? Is it one-to-one? Is it a homeomorphism? Can you use f to find a set which has the same cardinal number as the unit square?

7–4 The Index of a Transformation

Throughout this section X is a plane, and we consider transformations $f: X \to X$ (or perhaps $f: X_1 \to X$, where $X_1 \subset X$). A point which is its own image under the transformation (that is, a point $x \in X$ for which

FIGURE 4.1

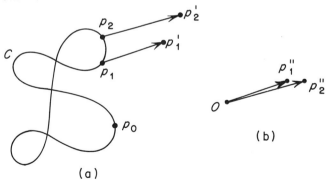

(a)

(b)

$f(x) = x$), is called a *fixed point* of f. Every point of X is a fixed point of the identity transformation, while a translation (not the identity) has no fixed points.

Let $f: X \to X$ be a continuous transformation and let C be an oriented closed curve in X which contains no fixed points of f (Fig. 4.1a). That is, C is a curve which begins at some point p_0, is traced out in a given sense, and ends at the same point p_0. For each point $p \in C$, set $f(p) = p'$; then pp' is a non-zero vector. Choose any convenient point $O \in X$ and draw a vector Op'' which is parallel, and equal in length, to pp'. (Fig. 4.1 shows the construction for two points p_1 and p_2.) Now imagine that the point p moves along the curve in the given sense, eventually returning to its original position. As p moves, the vector Op'' may rotate about O in either direction, but when p has completed one circuit around C and has returned to its original position, the vector Op'' will also have returned to its original position and will have made an integral number of complete revolutions about the point O. Let us describe rotations in the counter-clockwise direction as positive, and clockwise rotations as negative; then there is a unique integer n (positive, negative, or zero) which gives the number of rotations of Op'' about O as the point p moves once around the curve C. This integer n is called the *index of f along C* (in the given sense). Notice that the index of f along C is not defined if C contains a fixed point of f.

Example 4.1 Let C be a circle, oriented as in Fig. 4.2a, and let f be the trans-formation given by a counterclockwise rotation of 90 deg about the center of C. Several of the vectors pp' are shown in Fig. 4.2a. Figure 4.2b shows the cor-responding vectors Op''. The index of f along C is $+1$.

We want to show that certain deformations of an oriented closed curve C do not affect the index of a transformation along C; a rigorous proof of this fact is beyond the scope of this introductory text, but we shall be able to make the result seem plausible.

FIGURE 4.2

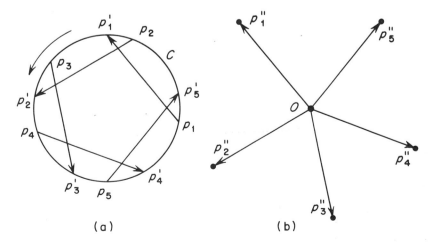

(a)   (b)

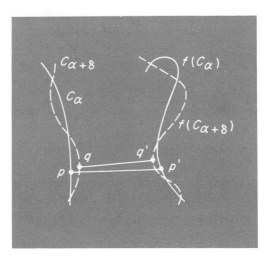

FIGURE 4.3

Theorem 4.1 If $f: X \to X$ is a continuous transformation, and if the oriented closed curve C_0 can be deformed into the oriented closed curve C_1 without passing over any fixed point of f, then the index of f along C_0 equals the index of f along C_1.

PROOF (of plausibility). As the curve C_0 is deformed into the curve C_1, it changes successively through an infinite number of positions (curves). We think of all these curves as being parametrized by a real number α, $0 \le \alpha \le 1$, so that, for each α in this range, we have a curve C_α, and the first and last of these curves (C_0 and C_1) are the curves of the theorem. We define a function n by setting $n(\alpha)$ equal to the index of f along C_α. Then the function n is defined for all values of α between 0 and 1 inclusive, and the values of this function are integers. Now if α is changed slightly, say to $\alpha + \delta$, the curve C_α changes slightly to the curve $C_{\alpha+\delta}$ (Fig. 4.3; only a portion of each of the curves is shown). An arbitrary point p on C_α moves to a point q on $C_{\alpha+\delta}$. But $f: X \to X$ is continuous, so the image curve also changes only slightly. Thus, for each vector pp', whose rotation gives the index of f along C, the vector qq' is in almost the same direction, and the rotation of this vector qq' gives the index of f along $C_{\alpha+\delta}$. Since at each point the directions of pp' and qq' are almost the same, the total amount of rotation of these two vectors must be nearly the same. But this total amount of rotation is an integral number of revolutions. Thus, since n can change only slightly, and is always an integer, it must remain constant; this is the desired conclusion «.

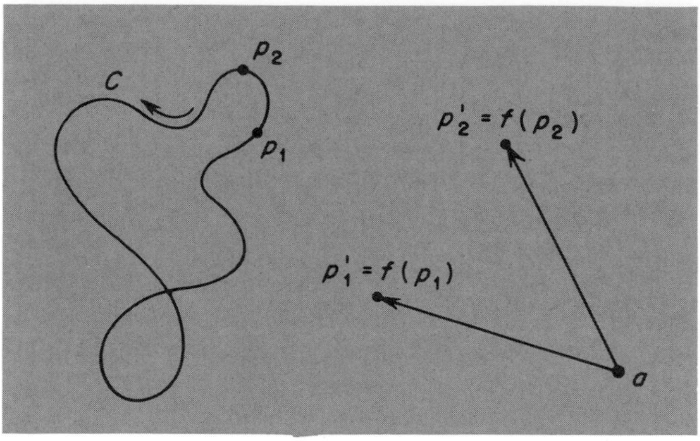

FIGURE 4.4

It is evident from the proof of Theorem 4.1 that f does not have to be defined on the entire plane X. It is sufficient for f to be defined on the portion of the plane which is used in deforming C_0 into C_1. This case will arise in the applications in Section 7-5.

We have been discussing the index of a transformation along an oriented closed curve C; there is another related concept which we shall describe. Let $f: X \to X$ be a continuous transformation; let C be an oriented closed curve in X (Fig. 4.4), and let $a \in X$ be a point which is not contained in the image of C under f; that is, $a \notin f(C)$. For each point $p \in C$, determine the vector from a to the point $p' = f(p)$ (Fig. 4.4 shows the construction for two points). Now imagine that the point p moves along the curve C in the given sense, eventually returning to its original position. As p moves, the vector ap' may rotate about a in either direction, but when p has completed one circuit around C and has returned to its original position the vector ap' will also have returned to its original position and will have made an integral number of complete revolutions about a. This number of revolutions (positive if counter-clockwise, negative if clockwise) is the *index of f at the point a with respect to the curve C* (in the given sense).

Theorem 4.2 Let $f: X \to X$ be a continuous transformation and let a be a point of X. If the oriented closed curve C_0 can be deformed into the oriented closed curve C_1 without passing over any point in $f^{-1}(a)$, then the index of f at a with respect to C_0 equals the index of f at a with respect to C_1.

PROOF. Problem 5 **«**.

The two indices of transformations which have been defined in this section will be used in Section 7-5 to prove two important results.

PROBLEMS

1. For each of the following transformations $f: X \to X$, find the index of f along the circle with center at the origin and radius 1. Orient the circle in the counterclockwise direction.

(**a**) A translation (Example 3.2a).

(**b**) A rotation (Example 3.2b).

(**c**) A stretching (Example 3.2c).

(**d**) Let O be the origin, and define $f(x) = O$ for every $x \in X$.

(**e**) Let a be the point $(10, 15)$ (in rectangular coordinates), and define $f(x) = a$ for every $x \in X$.

(**f**) The two transformations which send the point with polar coordinates (r, θ) into the point with polar coordinates $(kr, 2\theta)$; $k = \frac{1}{2}, 2$.

(**g**) The transformation which sends the point with polar coordinates (r, s) into the point with rectangular coordinates (r, s). (Hint: Be careful!)

2. What are the fixed points of the transformations of Problem 1?

3. Let $f: X \to X$ be a continuous transformation, and let C be an oriented curve in X (not necessarily closed) which contains no fixed points of f. Define an oriented closed curve C' by tracing the curve C and then retracing C in the reverse direction. Prove that the index of f along C' is zero.

#4. Let $f: X \to X$ be a continuous transformation and let a be a point of X such that $f(a) \neq a$. Show that if C is a circle in X with center a and sufficiently small radius, then the index of f along C is zero.

5. Prove Theorem 4.2.

6. (**a**) Find the index of a rotation at the origin with respect to the unit circle (center at the origin, radius 1, oriented counter clockwise).

(**b**) Find the index of a rotation at the point $(10, 15)$ (rectangular coordinates) with respect to the unit circle.

(**c**) Find the indices of the transformations of Problem 1(f) at the origin with respect to the unit circle.

(**d**) Find the indices of the transformations of Problem 1(f) at the point $(10, 15)$ (rectangular coordinates) with respect to the unit circle.

#(e) Let $f: X \to X$ be the transformation which sends the point with polar coordinates (r, θ) into the point with polar coordinates $(r^n, n\theta)$. Find the index of f at the origin with respect to the unit circle. [*Ans.: n.*]

#7. Prove that the index of f at a with respect to the oriented closed curve C is the same as the index of the identity transformation at a with respect to the curve $f(C)$.

8. Criticize the proof of Theorem 4.1. Why is it only a "proof of plausibility"? Where did we use the hypothesis that, in the deformation, the curve does not pass over any fixed point of f?

7–5 Applications of Indices of Transformations

We have found (Section 7-4, Problem 2) that a continuous transformation may, or may not, have a fixed point. In this section we shall use the concept of the index of a transformation to prove a remarkable theorem due to the Dutch mathematician L. E. J. Brouwer (1881-) which says that certain transformations must have a fixed point. We shall also give a proof of the fundamental theorem of algebra. The proofs of these two theorems will be based on the two different indices of transformations which were defined in Section 7-4.

Theorem 5.1 (Brouwer's fixed point theorem) If X is a closed disk, then every continuous transformation $f : X \to X$ has a fixed point.

PROOF. The proof is by contradiction. Let C_0 be the circumference of X and let C_1 be a circle concentric with C_0 and with radius r smaller than the radius of C_0. If f has no fixed points, then C_0 can be deformed into C_1 without passing over any fixed points of f, and, by Theorem 4.1, the indices of f along C_0 and C_1 must be the same. If r is sufficiently small, the index of f along C_1 is zero (Problem 4, Section 7-4). The proof will be completed by showing that the index of f along C_0 is not zero. In fact, at each point $p \in C_0$, the vector from p to $p' = f(p)$ must point into the disk (Fig. 5.1); that is, the vector pp' stays always on the same side of the tangent line to C at p. Evidently, when p makes one circuit around C, the tangent line to C makes exactly one revolution. Since the vector pp' stays always on the same side of the tangent, it must also make one revolution, and the index of f along C_0 is $+1$ or -1 **«**.

Let us say that a subset X of three-dimensional space has the _fixed point property_ iff every continuous transformation of X into itself has a fixed point. Then Brouwer's fixed point theorem states that a closed disk has the fixed point property. It is easy to see that a closed disk with the center point removed does not have this property (try a rotation); also, a sphere fails to have the fixed point property. Other examples appear in the problems.

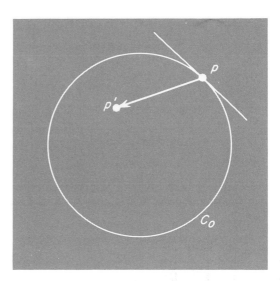

FIGURE 5.1

The proof of Theorem 5.1 was based on the concept of the index of a transformation along a curve. The proof of the following theorem will use the index of a transformation at a point with respect to a curve.

Theorem 5.2 (fundamental theorem of algebra) Every polynomial equation with coefficients which are complex numbers, and of degree $n > 0$, has at least one root among the complex numbers.

PROOF. We think of any complex number $u + iv$ as representing the point in a plane X whose rectangular coordinates are (u, v), and we define the absolute value of a complex number in the usual way as

$$|u + iv| = \sqrt{u^2 + v^2}.$$

Then, if z_1 and z_2 are any two complex numbers, the distance from the origin to z_1 is $|z_1|$, and the distance from the point z_1 to the point z_2 is $|z_2 - z_1|$.

Since we can divide through by the coefficient of the highest degree term, we may suppose that

$$f(z) = z^n + a_1 z^{n-1} + a_2 z^{n-2} + \cdots + a_{n-1} z + a_n$$

where $a_1, a_2, \ldots, a_n$ are complex numbers, and we must prove that the equation $f(z) = 0$ has at least one root.

The proof proceeds by contradiction. Suppose that $f(z) = 0$ has no roots; then $a_n \neq 0$, since otherwise zero would be a root of $f(z) = 0$.

FIGURE 5.2

Now under the continuous transformation $f:X \to X$, which sends the point z into the point $f(z)$, the origin is sent into the point a_n. Because f is continuous, all the points sufficiently near to the origin are sent into points which are near to a_n. Thus, the image of a small circle C_0 with center at the origin is a closed curve C lying near to a_n (Fig. 5.2). It follows that the index of f at the origin with respect to C_0 is zero. But C_0 can be enlarged to an arbitrarily large circle C_1 without passing over any point of $f^{-1}(0)$ ($f^{-1}(0)$ is empty, since $f(z) = 0$ has no roots); hence, by Theorem 4.2, the index of f at the origin with respect to C_1 is zero.

Now consider the transformation $g:X \to X$ defined by $g(z) = z^n$. By Problem 6(e), Section 7-4, the index of g at the origin with respect to the unit circle is n. Since $g^{-1}(0) = \{0\}$, the unit circle can be enlarged to the circle C_1 without passing over any point of $g^{-1}(0)$; hence, by Theorem 4.2, the index of g at the origin with respect to C_1 is n.

The proof by contradiction will be concluded by showing that the indices of f and g at the origin with respect to C_1 are the same. By Problem 7, Section 7-4, it suffices to show that the indices of the identity transformation $i:X \to X$ ($i(z) = z$ for every $z \in X$) at the origin with respect to the two curves $f(C_1)$ and $g(C_1)$ are the same. This result will follow from Theorem 4.2 if we show that the curve $f(C_1)$ can be deformed into the curve $g(C_1)$ without passing through the origin ($i^{-1}(0) = \{0\}$). Such a deformation is described in the next paragraph.

Choose the radius R of C_1 so that

$$R > 1, \quad \text{and} \quad R > |a_1| + |a_2| + \cdots + |a_n|.$$

For any point $z \in C_1$, the distance from $f(z)$ to $g(z)$ is $|f(z) - g(z)|$ and we find

$$|f(z) - g(z)| = |a_1 z^{n-1} + a_2 z^{n-2} + \cdots + a_{n-1} z + a_n|$$
$$\leq |a_1| R^{n-1} + |a_2| R^{n-2} + \cdots + |a_{n-1}| R + |a_n|$$
$$\leq R^{n-1}[|a_1| + |a_2| + \cdots + |a_n|] < R^n = |g(z)|.$$

Thus, for any $z \in C_1$, the distance between $f(z)$ and $g(z)$ is less than the distance from $g(z)$ to the origin, so the origin cannot be on the line segment from $f(z)$ to $g(z)$. But this means that the curve $f(C_1)$ can be deformed into the curve $g(C_1)$ by moving each point $f(z) \in f(C_1)$ along the line segment joining $f(z)$ to $g(z)$, and, during this deformation, the curve will never pass through the origin **.

PROBLEMS

1. Prove that none of the following subsets of three-dimensional space has the fixed point property.
   (a) A torus.
   (b) A sphere.
   (c) An open disk.
   (d) A closed disk with a single point of the open disk removed.
   (e) A closed disk with a single point of the circumference removed.

2. (a) Examine several examples of continuous transformations of a closed disk into itself and find a fixed point for each. Can there be more than one fixed point? Can there be any number of fixed points?
   (b) Find a homeomorphism of a sphere onto itself with no fixed points; with exactly one fixed point; with exactly two fixed points.

3. Give an alternative proof of Brouwer's fixed point theorem based on the following: Let $f: X \to X$ be a continuous transformation of a closed disk into itself which has no fixed points. For each point $x \in X$, draw the line segment from $f(x)$ to x and extend this segment until it meets the circumference in the point x'. Define a transformation $g: X \to X$ by setting $g(x) = x'$. Then g is a continuous transformation which transforms the closed disk onto its circumference and leaves each point of the circumference fixed. But it is intuitively evident that there is no such transformation as g.

*4. Prove that if f is a continuous transformation of a sphere S into itself, then either f has a fixed point or there is some point which f sends into its diametrically opposite point. (Hint: Suppose f has no fixed points, and sends no point into its diametrically opposite point. Determine a unique direction d at each point $p \in S$ by taking the tangent to the shorter arc of the great circle joining p to $f(p)$. Now consider any directed circle C on S (Fig. 5.3). At each point $p \in C$ let θ be the angle between the vector t which is tangent to C at p and the direction d determined as above. As p moves once around C, the net change in the angle θ will be an integral multiple of 360 deg. Call this integral multiple the index of C. By a proof similar to that of Theorem 4.1, prove that deforming a circular curve does not change its index. A contradiction is reached by starting with a very small circle C_0 and subjecting it to two different deformations: (1) Slide C_0 around to the diametrically opposite position C_1 on the sphere, keeping the size of C_0 constant; (2) expand C_0 to a great circle and contract in the other hemisphere to obtain the same final circle C_1 as in deformation (1). Prove that under at least one of these deformations the index of the circle must change.)

5. Prove that if hair grew all over a billiard ball, it would be impossible to comb it without a cowlick. (Hint: Use Problem 4.)

6. Prove that if $f:S \to S$ and $g:S \to S$ are two continuous transformations of a sphere S into itself, then at least one of the transformations f, g, and $g \bigcirc f$ has a fixed point. [Remember $(g \bigcirc f)(x) = g(f(x))$.] (Hint: If not, then for each point $p \in S$, the three points p, $p' = f(p)$, and $p'' = g(p')$ are distinct. These three points determine a unique circle. Use this circle to define a continuous transformation $h:S \to S$ with no fixed points and no point sent into its diametrically opposite point. This contradicts the result of Problem 4.)

7. As a special case of the result of Problem 6, prove that if $f:S \to S$ is a continuous transformation of a sphere into itself, then either f has a fixed point or there are two distinct points p and q of S such that $f(p) = q$ and $f(q) = p$.

8. Draw figures illustrating the proof of Theorem 5.2 for the case where $f(z) = z^2 + 2z + 2$.

9. In the proof of Theorem 5.2 it was stated that the transformations f and g are continuous. Prove this fact. (Hint: Define addition and multiplication of two points z_1 and z_2 in a plane, and generalize the proof of Theorem 3.1 to the case where X is a plane.)

FIGURE 5.3

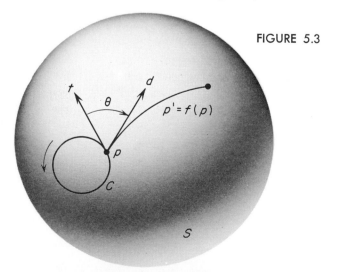

E I G H T

Spaces

8-1 Introduction

In Chapter 7 we have seen how the concept of
the distance between two points in three-dimensional space can be used to define continuity of
transformations; this concept, in turn, was used
to define topological equivalence of figures. But
we have also discussed some figures (for example,
the Klein bottle) which are not subsets of three-
dimensional Euclidean space. The definitions
of continuity and topological equivalence can be
generalized so that they are applicable in these
situations. The generalization is made in this
chapter.

In Section 8-2 we show that the concept of the distance between two points may be available even when the "points" are elements of an arbitrary set (perhaps a set of functions). In this case, we speak of the set as a metric space; the definitions of continuity and topological equivalence can be carried over to metric spaces immediately from their statements in Chapter 7.

In Section 8-3 we shall find that some of the concepts which can be defined in a metric space (e.g., open set, closed set) may be available in still more general situations. These concepts will be used to define continuity and topological equivalence in these more general situations.

Three particularly important properties (connectedness, compactness, and completeness) are discussed in Sections 8-4, 8-5, and 8-6. The first two are topological properties; the last is not.

8–2 Metric Spaces

In Section 7-3 we mentioned four basic properties of the distance function in three-dimensional space. We shall see here that, if X is any set and d is a function which has these properties, then many of the concepts of interest in connection with three-dimensional space can be defined in the set X.

Let X be a set, and let d be a real-valued function defined for pairs of points $x \in X$, $y \in X$. The function d is a *metric* in X if and only if the following conditions are satisfied for all points x, y, and z of X.

(1) $d(x, y) \geq 0$.

(2) $d(x, y) = 0$, iff $x = y$.

(3) $d(x, y) = d(y, x)$.

(4) $d(x, y) + d(y, z) \geq d(x, z)$.

The value of the function d at the points x, y [i.e., the real number $d(x, y)$] is called the *distance* from x to y. A *metric space* is a set X together with a metric d in X.

Before we discuss metric spaces, let us look at some examples. Each of Examples 2.1 through 2.6 is a metric space.

Example 2.1 X is any subset of three-dimensional Euclidean space; $d(x, y)$ is the ordinary distance from x to y.

Example 2.2 X is an arbitrary set; the function d is defined by setting

$$d(x, y) = \begin{cases} 0, & \text{if } x = y. \\ 1, & \text{if } x \neq y. \end{cases}$$

Example 2.3 X is the set of all points in a plane; for any points $x = (x_1, x_2) \in X$ and $y = (y_1, y_2) \in X$, set

$$d(x, y) = |x_1 - y_1| + |x_2 - y_2|.$$

Example 2.4 X is the set of all continuous real-valued functions defined on the unit interval

$$I = \{t : 0 \leq t \leq 1\};$$

for any two functions $x \in X$ and $y \in X$, set

$$d(x, y) = \max_{t \in I} |x(t) - y(t)|.$$

Example 2.5 X is the same as in Example 4;

$$d(x, y) = \int_0^1 |x(t) - y(t)| \, dt.$$

Example 2.6 X is the set of all ordered n-tuples of real numbers. For any two ordered n-tuples

$$x = (x_1, x_2, \ldots, x_n) \in X \quad \text{and} \quad y = (y_1, y_2, \ldots, y_n) \in X,$$

set

$$d(x, y) = \max_{0 \leq i \leq n} |x_i - y_i|.$$

Each of Examples 2.7 through 2.10 is *not* a metric space.

Example 2.7 X is the set of all real numbers;

$$d(x, y) = x^2 - y^2.$$

Example 2.8 X is the set of all real numbers;

$$d(x, y) = |x^2 - y^2|.$$

Example 2.9 X is the set of all real numbers;

$$d(x, y) = \begin{cases} x - y, & \text{if } x \geq y. \\ 1, & \text{if } x < y. \end{cases}$$

Example 2.10 X is the set of all points along a certain river bank (fixed relative to the earth, not moving with the river). For any two points $x \in X$ and $y \in X$, set $d(x, y)$ equal to the time required to row from x to y.

Any definitions which depend only on the concept of distance can be generalized immediately to apply to arbitrary metric spaces. For completeness, we state below the ones in which we shall be most interested.

Let X and Y be metric spaces with metrics d and e respectively. The points $x_1 \in X$ and $x_2 \in X$ are *δ-near* iff $d(x_1, x_2) < \delta$. Similarly, $y_1 \in Y$ is *ε-near* to $y_2 \in Y$ iff $e(y_1, y_2) < \varepsilon$. A transformation $f: X \to Y$ is *continuous at $x_0 \in X$* iff for every $\varepsilon > 0$ there is a $\delta > 0$ such that, if x is δ-near to x_0, then $f(x)$ is ε-near to $f(x_0)$. The transformation f is *continuous* iff it is continuous at every point of X. A *homeomorphism* is a continuous transformation which has a continuous inverse transformation. The *open ball* with center $x_0 \in X$ and radius $r > 0$ is the set

$$B(x_0; r) = \{x: x \in X, \quad \text{and} \quad d(x_0, x) < r\}.$$

An open ball is called an open sphere by some authors, but we shall reserve the term "sphere" for the set

$$\{x: d(x_0, x) = r\}.$$

The *closed ball* with center $x_0 \in X$ and radius $r > 0$ (denoted by $B^-(x_0; r)$) is the set

$$B^-(x_0; r) = \{x: x \in X \quad \text{and} \quad d(x_0, x) \leq r\}.$$

Example 2.11 In the space X of Example 2.4, let $x_0 \in X$ be the function which is identically zero; that is, $x_0(t) = 0$ for all values of $t \in I$. The open ball $B(x_0; 1)$ is composed of all functions $x \in X$ whose graphs lie in the rectangle shown in Fig. 2.1.

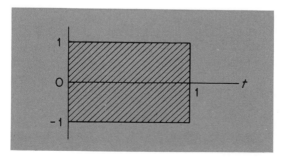

FIGURE 2.1

Example 2.12 In the space X of Example 2.5, let $x_0 \in X$ be the function which is identically zero; that is, $x_0(t) = 0$ for all $t \in I$. The open ball $B(x_0; 1)$ is the set composed of all the functions $x \in X$ such that the area bounded by the curves

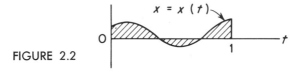

FIGURE 2.2

$x = x(t)$ and the lines $x = 0$, $t = 0$, $t = 1$ is less than 1. Figure 2.2 shows one such area; note that the area below the t-axis is *not* counted as being negative.

The reader should prove the following theorem as an exercise; this result will be used in proving later theorems.

Theorem 2.1 A transformation $f:X \to Y$ is continuous iff, for every $x_1 \in X$ and every open ball

$$B_1 = B(f(x_1); \varepsilon) \subset Y$$

with center $f(x_1)$, there is an open ball

$$B_2 = B(x_1; \delta) \subset X$$

with center x_1 such that $B_2 \subset f^{-1}(B_1)$.

PROOF. Exercise «.

Theorem 2.2 Let X and Y be metric spaces with metrics d and e respectively; a necessary and sufficient condition that $f:X \to Y$ be continuous is that if B_1 is an open ball in Y such that $x \in f^{-1}(B_1)$, then there is an open ball $B_2 \subset X$ such that $x \in B_2 \subset f^{-1}(B_1)$.

PROOF. *Sufficiency:* Suppose that the condition of the theorem is satisfied and let $B_1 = B(f(x_1); \varepsilon)$ be an open ball in Y with center $f(x_1)$. Then $x_1 \in f^{-1}(B_1)$, so there is some open ball $B_2 = B(x_2; r)$ in X such that $x_1 \in B_2 \subset f^{-1}(B_1)$. Set $\delta = r - d(x_2, x_1)$; since $x_1 \in B_2$, $\delta > 0$. Let $B_2^* = B(x_1; \delta)$; then B_2^* is an open ball with center x_1. If $x \in B_2^*$, then

$$d(x_2, x) \le d(x_2, x_1) + d(x_1, x) \le d(x_2, x_1) + \delta = r,$$

so $x \in B_2$. Thus $B_2^* \subset B_2 \subset f^{-1}(B_1)$. Therefore, by Theorem 2.1, f is continuous.

Necessity: If f is continuous, then the condition of Theorem 2.1 is satisfied. Suppose that $B_1 = B(y_1; r)$ is an open ball in Y and $x \in f^{-1}(B_1)$. Then $f(x) \in B_1$, so that

$$\varepsilon = r - e(y_1, f(x)) > 0.$$

Set $B_0 = B(f(x); \varepsilon)$; it follows from the triangle inequality that $B_0 \subset B_1$. But by Theorem 2.1 there is an open ball $B_2 = B(x; \delta) \subset X$, with center x, such that

$$B_2 \subset f^{-1}(B_0) \subset f^{-1}(B_1).$$

Certainly $x \in B_2$.«

Two concepts which we have not previously discussed are defined below; these definitions are applicable in any metric space. We shall see later that these concepts may be meaningful in more general situations. In fact, one of them will form the basis of our generalization from metric spaces to topological spaces in Section 8-3.

A subset U of a metric space X is *open* iff, for each point $x \in U$, there is an open ball B such that $x \in B \subset U$. A subset $F \subset X$ is *closed* iff F' is open.

If U is open and $x \in U$, there is a ball B_1 such that $x \in B_1 \subset U$. But then there is a ball B_2 with center x such that $B_2 \subset B_1$. Thus, a set $U \subset X$ is open iff, for each $x \in U$, there is a ball $B(x; r) \subset U$. This form of the definition shows why the word "open" was chosen to describe this concept; it is in the sense of "wide open spaces." If U is open and $x \in U$, then U also contains any point that is sufficiently near to x. That is, intuitively, x cannot be on the "edge" of U in the sense of having some point very near to x be outside of U. The intuitive meaning of the word "closed" is a little more difficult to describe. We shall see later that it can be interpreted in the sense of "enclosed" or "containing a fence around it."

It is easy to see that there are sets which are neither open nor closed. In the metric space composed of the real numbers (Example 1), let $A = \{x : x \text{ is rational}\}$ and $B = \{x : x \text{ is irrational}\}$. Then neither A nor B is an open set; but A and B are complements, so neither one is closed. A more surprising result is that there are some sets which are both open and closed. In fact, in Example 2.2, it is easy to see that $B(x; \frac{1}{2}) = \{x\}$; that is, each open ball of radius $\frac{1}{2}$ contains exactly one point. In this metric space, every set is open, and, consequently, every set is also closed. This is an extreme example, but, in any metric space X, the empty set $\emptyset$ and the whole space X are both open and closed.

Theorem 2.3 The transformation $f: X \to Y$ from the metric space X into the metric space Y is continuous iff, for every open set $V \subset Y$, the set $f^{-1}(V)$ is open.

PROOF. *Necessity:* Let f be continuous, let V be an open subset of Y, and let x be a point of $f^{-1}(V)$; to show that $f^{-1}(V)$ is open, we shall find an open ball B such that $x \in B \subset f^{-1}(V)$. Since $f(x) \in V$, there is an open ball B_1 with $f(x) \in B_1 \subset V$. But then $x \in f^{-1}(B_1)$, and, by Theorem 2.2, there is an open ball $B \subset X$ such that

$$x \in B \subset f^{-1}(B_1) \subset f^{-1}(V).$$

Sufficiency: Let B_1 be an open ball in Y and let x be a point of $f^{-1}(B_1)$. Since B_1 is an open ball, it is open (Problem 9); hence, by the condition of the theorem, $f^{-1}(B_1)$ is also open. Since x is a point of the open set $f^{-1}(B_1)$, there is an open ball B_2 such that $x \in B_2 \subset f^{-1}(B_1)$ and, by Theorem 2.2, f is continuous «.

Theorems 2.2 and 2.3 give two characterizations of continuous trans-formations between metric spaces. The condition of Theorem 2.2 is usually more convenient to use, but, in more general spaces, this condition will become meaningless and the condition of Theorem 2.3 will be the important one.

PROBLEMS

1. (a) Prove that each of Examples 2.1 through 2.6 is a metric space.
   (b) Prove that each of Examples 2.7 through 2.10 is not a metric space.

2. Which of the following examples are metric spaces?
   (a) The set X is the set of all the real numbers; for $x \in X$ and $y \in X$, set $d(x, y) = |x - y|$.
   (b) The set X is the set of real numbers; for $x \in X$ and $y \in X$, set $d(x, y) = (x^y - y^x)^2$.
   (c) The set X is a plane; for $x = (x_1, x_2) \in X$ and $y = (y_1, y_2) \in X$, set

   $$d(x, y) = \max \{|x_1 - y_1|, |x_2 - y_2|\}.$$

   (d) The set X is a plane; for $x = (x_1, x_2) \in X$ and $y = (y_1, y_2) \in X$, set

   $$d(x, y) = \begin{cases} [(x_1 - y_1)^2 + (x_2 - y_2)^2]^{1/2}, & \text{if } x_1 \neq y_1 \\ 1, & \text{if } x_1 = y_1 \text{ and } x_2 \neq y_2 \\ 0, & \text{if } x_1 = y_1 \text{ and } x_2 = y_2. \end{cases}$$

3. Prove that a real-valued function d defined for pairs of points $x \in X$, $y \in X$ is a metric in X if and only if d satisfies the two conditions
(a) $d(x, y) = 0$ iff $x = y$.
(b) $d(x, y) \le d(x, z) + d(y, z)$.

4. Let i be the identity transformation from the metric space of Example 2.4 to the metric space of Example 2.5. Prove that i is continuous. Is i^{-1} continuous?

5. (a) Let X be the metric space of Example 2.4 and define a transformation $f: X \to X$ by setting $f(x) = y$ where

$$y(t) = \int_0^t x(t)\, dt.$$

Is f continuous?
(b) Do the problem in part (a) if X is the metric space of Example 2.5.

6. Prove that a necessary and sufficient condition that $f: X \to Y$ be continuous. is that for every $x_1 \in X$ and for every open ball $B_1 = B(f(x_1); \epsilon) \subset Y$, with center $f(x_1)$, there is an open ball $B_2 = B(x_1; \delta) \subset X$, with center x_1, such that $B_2 \subset f^{-1}(B_1)$.

7. Compare the statement of Theorem 2.2 with the statement of Problem 5 of Section 7-3. Why was it necessary for the statement in the problem to be more complicated than the statement in the theorem?

8. Prove that, in any metric space X, each of the sets $\emptyset$ and X is both open and closed.

9. Show that an open ball is open; show also that a closed ball is closed.

10. (a) Show that the intersection of any two open sets is open.
(b) Show that the intersection of any finite number of open sets is open.
(c) Show that the union of any family (not necessarily finite) of open sets is open.

#11. (a) Show that the intersection of any family of closed sets is closed.
(b) Show that the union of any finite number of closed sets is closed.

12. Prove that a transformation $f: X \to Y$ between two metric spaces is continuous iff, for every closed subset F of Y, $f^{-1}(F)$ is a closed subset of X.

13. Let X and Y be the metric spaces of Example 2.2 and Problem 2(a) respectively. Which of the following transformations $f: X \to Y$ are continuous? Which have a continuous inverse? (Take X as the real numbers.)
(a) $f(x) = x$
(b) $f(x) = 2x$
(c) $f(x) = x^2$

14. Do Problem 13 for the transformations $f: Y \to X$.

15. Let X and Y be the metric spaces of Examples 2.4 and 2.5 respectively. Which of the following transformations $f: X \to Y$ are continuous? Which have a continuous inverse?

   (a) $f(x(t)) = x(t)$
   (b) $f(x(t)) = 2x(t)$
   (c) $f(x(t)) = [x(t)]^2$
   (d) $f(x(t)) = x(t^2)$

16. Do Problem 15 for the transformations $f: Y \to X$.

We shall discuss two more concepts, closure and convergence, in metric spaces before we consider more general spaces in the next section.

For any subset A of a metric space S, the *closure* of A, denoted by A^-, is the smallest closed set having A as a subset. That is,

   (i) A^- is closed.
   (ii) $A^- \supset A$.
   (iii) If F is closed and $F \supset A$, then $F \supset A^-$.

It is easy to see that each set $A \subset X$ has a closure; that is, there always exists a smallest closed set having A as a subset. For, consider the family $\mathcal{F}$ of all closed sets which have A as a subset (the set X is certainly a member of this family). By Problem 11a above, the intersection of all the sets in this family is a closed set. This intersection will have A as a subset and will certainly be the smallest closed set which has A as a subset. Thus we see that the closure of A is the intersection of all the closed sets which have A as a subset. That is,

$$A^- = \cap \, \{F : F \text{ is closed} \quad \text{and} \quad F \supset A\}.$$

Theorem 2.4 A point $x \in X$ is in the closure of a subset $A \subset X$ if and only if each open ball $B(x; r)$ has at least one point in common with A; that is,

$$A \cap B(x; r) \neq \emptyset.$$

PROOF. Suppose $x \notin A^-$; then $x \in (A^-)'$. But $(A^-)'$ is an open set; hence, there is an open ball B_1 such that $x \in B_1 \subset (A^-)'$. Since $x \in B_1$, there is an open ball B, with center at x, such that $B \subset B_1$, and we have

$$B \subset B_1 \subset (A^-)' \subset A'.$$

Thus $A \cap B = \emptyset$.
   Suppose there is an open ball $B = B(x; r)$ such that $A \cap B = \emptyset$.

Then B' is one of the closed sets having A as a subset, so $A^- \subset B'$. Since $x \in B$, it follows that $x \notin A^-$. «

Theorem 2.4 shows that the closure of a set A consists of all the points which are very near to points of A; more exactly, $x \in A^-$ iff, for every $\varepsilon > 0$, there is a point of A which is ε-near to x.

We have seen that any subset $A \subset X$ determines a subset A^- called the closure of A, This means that closure is a unary operation on the subsets of X. The next theorem gives the most important properties of this operation.

Theorem 2.5 For any subsets S and T of X,

(a) $\emptyset^- = \emptyset$.   (c) $S^{--} = S^-$.

(b) $S^- \supset S$.   (d) $S^- \cup T^- = (S \cup T)^-$.

PROOF. (a) Since $\emptyset$ is closed and is a subset of every set, it is evidently the smallest closed set having $\emptyset$ as a subset. That is, $\emptyset^- = \emptyset$.

(b) This is evident from the definition of closure.

(c) Since S^- is itself closed, it is one of the closed sets having S^- as a subset. Evidently, it is the smallest closed set having S^- as a subset; i.e., $S^{--} = S^-$.

(d) The set $(S \cup T)^-$ is one of the closed sets having S as a subset; hence $S^- \subset (S \cup T)^-$. Similarly, $T^- \subset (S \cup T)^-$, and these two inclusions imply that

$$S^- \cup T^- \subset (S \cup T)^-.$$

For the other inclusion, notice that S^- is a closed set having S as a subset, and T^- is a closed set having T as a subset. Thus, $S^- \cup T^-$ is a closed set (Problem 11b above) having $S \cup T$ as a subset. That is, $S^- \cup T^- \supset (S \cup T)^-$. «

Example 2.13 Let X be the metric space of Example 2.4, and let S be the set of all functions $x \in X$ such that the graph of x consists of a finite number of line segments. Let $x_2 \in X$ be the function defined by $x_2(t) = t^2$ for $t \in I$. Then $x_2 \in S^-$. This can be seen in Fig. 2.3, which shows the graph of the function x_2 and a strip of vertical dimension 2ε about this graph. Evidently, for any $x \in S$, $d(x_2, x) < \varepsilon$ iff the graph of x lies in this strip; Fig. 2.3 shows that there is at least one $x \in S$ which satisfies this condition. Thus, for any ε, the open ball $B(x_2; \varepsilon)$ has at least one element in common with S so that, by Theorem 2.4, $x_2 \in S^-$.

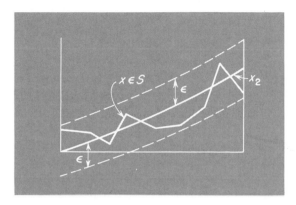

FIGURE 2.3

Having gained some acquaintance with the concept of closure, we turn now to convergence, which, as we shall see, is a closely related concept. We shall confine our attention to convergence of sequences.

A *sequence* in a set X is a transformation from the set $N = \{1, 2, 3, \ldots\}$ into X. The notation used for sequences is somewhat different from that for general transformations. Instead of denoting the transformation by a letter, such as f, and the image of an element $n \in N$ by $f(n)$, we shall follow the usual custom and indicate the image of $n \in N$ by using a subscript notation, such as x_n, and shall denote the sequence (transformation) by $(x_1, x_2, x_3, \ldots)$ or, more briefly by (x_n). The value x_n of the function is called the *nth term* of the sequence. Of course, it may happen that $x_i = x_j$ for certain distinct values of i and j. For example, $(p, p, p, \ldots)$ is a sequence in the set $\{p\}$; here

$$x_i = p \quad \text{for} \quad i = 1, 2, \ldots .$$

We shall be interested in sequences in a metric space X.

Suppose $A \subset X$ and (x_n) is a sequence in X. The sequence (x_n) is *eventually* in A iff there is an $n_0 \in N$ such that, for $n \geq n_0$, $x_n \in A$; that is, there is some term in the sequence (the n_0th) such that all of the later terms of the sequence lie in A. The sequence (x_n) is *frequently* in A iff, for every $n_0 \in N$, there is an $n \geq n_0$ such that $x_n \in A$. This condition is equivalent to the requirement that an infinite number of terms of the sequence are elements of A.

A sequence (x_n) in a metric space X *converges* to a point $x \in X$ if and only if for each open ball $B(x; r)$ with center x, the sequence is eventually in $B(x; r)$. We write $x_n \to x$, or $\lim x_n = x$, to denote that (x_n) converges to x, and we call x a limit point of the sequence (x_n) in this case.

Example 2.14 Let X be the set of real numbers and, for $x \in X$, $y \in X$, define

$$d(x, y) = |x - y|.$$

(a) Set

$$x_n = (-1)^n(1/n), \qquad n = 1, 2, \ldots.$$

For any open ball B with center at $x = 0$, the sequence (x_n) is eventually in B; consequently, (x_n) converges to 0. If $A = \{x : x > 0\}$ is the set of all positive real numbers, the sequence (x_n) is frequently (but not eventually) in A.

(b) Set

$$x_n = (-1)^n n, \qquad n = 1, 2, \ldots.$$

This sequence is frequently in the positive numbers, but does not converge to any point.

Example 2.15 (a) Let X be the metric space of Example 2.4 and let x_n ($n = 2, 3, 4, \ldots$) be the function whose graph is shown in Fig. 2.4. The

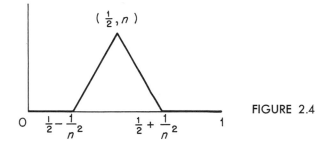

FIGURE 2.4

sequence (x_n) does not converge to any point $x \in X$. This can be seen by noticing that for any $x \in X$,

$$d(x, x_n) = \max_{t \in I} |x(t) - x_n(t)| \geq |x(\tfrac{1}{2}) - x_n(\tfrac{1}{2})| = |x(\tfrac{1}{2}) - n|.$$

Thus, for $n > x(\tfrac{1}{2}) + 1$, $d(x, x_n) > 1$ and (x_n) is eventually outside the open ball $B(x; 1)$.

(b) Let X be the metric space of Example 2.5 and let x_n ($n = 2, 3, 4, \ldots$) be the function whose graph is shown in Fig. 2.4. Then $x_n \to x_0$ where $x_0(t) = 0$ for all $t \in I$. In fact,

$$d(x_0, x_n) = \int_0^1 |x_0(t) - x_n(t)| \, dt = 1/n.$$

It follows that for any open ball B with center x_0, the sequence (x_n) is eventually in B.

As might be expected, the metric space where X is the set of real numbers and

$$d(x_1, x_2) = |x_1 - x_2|$$

is a special case of considerable importance. In fact, convergence of sequences in any metric space can be described in terms of convergence in this space. Let Y be a metric space with distance function e and let (y_n) be a sequence in Y. Then $y_n \to y_0 \in Y$ iff the sequence (y_n) is eventually in each open ball with center y_0. That is, iff for any real number $r > 0$, the sequence of real numbers $(e(y_0, y_n))$ is eventually in the set

$$A_r = \{x : 0 \le x < r\}.$$

This condition is necessary and sufficient for the sequence $(e(y_0, y_n))$ of real numbers to converge to zero in the metric space X. Thus, convergence of sequences in the arbitrary metric space Y can be described in terms of convergence to zero in the metric space X.

The following theorem gives the connection between convergence and closure.

Theorem 2.6 Let X be a metric space and let $S \subset X$; a point $x \in X$ is an element of S^- if and only if there is a sequence (x_n) in S which converges to x.

PROOF. If $x \in S^-$, then each open ball with center x intersects S. Choose

$$x_n \in S \cap B(x; 1/n).$$

Then the sequence (x_n) is eventually in each open ball with center x; hence, $x_n \to x$.

If there is a sequence (x_n) in S which converges to x, then this sequence is eventually in each open ball with center x; so certainly each of these open balls intersects S. Thus $x \in S^-$. «

Theorem 2.6 points up the intuitive connotations carried by the term "closed set." A set A is closed if and only if $A = A^-$ (Problem 17); by Theorem 2.6, this is the case iff, whenever a sequence (x_n) of points in A converges to a point x, the point x must be in A. Intuitively, the sequence (x_n) converges to x iff the points x_n get "very close" to x, so the condition that A be closed can be phrased as follows: Any point which is "very close" to points of A is a point of A. Again: It is not possible to sneak along a sequence of points in A and get "very close" to a point that is not in A. The points of A are enclosed — it is impossible to escape from them by sneaking along a sequence of points in A.

PROBLEMS (continued)

17. Let A be a subset of a metric space.
   (a) Prove that A is closed iff $A = A^-$.
   (b) Prove that A is closed iff A is the closure of some set.
   (c) Prove that if $A \subset B$ then $A^- \subset B^-$.

18. (a) If S and T are subsets of a metric space, how is the set $S^- \cap T^-$ related to the set $(S \cap T)^-$?
   (b) How is $(S^-)'$ related to $(S')^-$?
   (c) Give an example of an open ball $B(x; r)$ whose closure is different from the closed ball $B^-(x; r)$.

#19. Let X be a metric space.
   (a) If $p \in X$ and

$$x_n = p, \qquad n = 1, 2, 3, \ldots,$$

prove that $x_n \to p$.
   (b) If $x_n \to x_0$ and $n_1 < n_2 < n_3 < \ldots$, prove that the sequence $(x_{n_1}, x_{n_2}, x_{n_3}, \ldots)$ converges to x_0. The sequence $(x_{n_1}, x_{n_2}, x_{n_3}, \ldots)$ is called a *subsequence* of the sequence (x_n).
   (c) Prove that (x_n) has a subsequence which converges to x_0 iff (x_n) is frequently in each open ball $B(x_0; r)$ with center x_0.
   (d) Prove that if $x_n \to x$ and $x_n \to y$, then $x = y$.

20. Let (x_n) be a sequence in X and let A be a subset of X. Prove that (x_n) is eventually in A iff it is false that (x_n) is frequently in A'.

21. Let X be the set of real numbers and, for $x \in X, y \in X$, set

$$d(x, y) = |x - y|.$$

Find the closure of each of the following subsets of X.
   (a) $A = \{1, 2, 3, \ldots\}$.
   (b) $B = \{1, \frac{1}{2}, \frac{1}{3}, \ldots\}$.
   (c) $C = \{1, -\frac{1}{2}, \frac{1}{3}, -\frac{1}{4}, \ldots\}$.
   (d) $D = \{1, \frac{1}{2}, 3, \frac{1}{4}, 5, \ldots\}$.
   (e) $E = \{x : 0 < x < 1\}$.
   (f) $F = \{x : x \text{ is rational}\}$.
   (g) $G = \{x : x \text{ is irrational}\}$.

22. For each of the sets A to G in Problem 21, choose several points in the closure of the set and, for each point x which you choose, find a sequence in the set which converges to x. This process checks the result in Theorem 2.6.

23. (a) Let X be the metric space of Example 2.4, and let $x_n \in X$ be the function defined by $x_n(t) = t^n$ for all $t \in I$. Does the sequence (x_n) converge? If so, what is its limit?

(b) Do part (a) for the metric space of Example 2.5.

24. Let X be the set of real numbers and, for $x \in X$, $y \in X$, set

$$d(x, y) = \begin{cases} 0, & \text{if } x = y. \\ 1, & \text{if } x \neq y. \end{cases}$$

Describe convergence in this metric space; that is, tell which sequences converge to which points. What can you say about the closure of a set A in this space?

*25. Let $X - \{0, 1, 2, \ldots\}$ be the set of non-negative integers, and define a function d as follows: For

$$x \in X, \qquad y \in X, \qquad x \neq y,$$

let b be the biggest non-negative integer such that 2^b is a factor of $|x - y|$, then

$$d(x, y) = \frac{1}{b+1}, \qquad d(x, x) = 0.$$

(a) Find: (i) $d(0, 2)$, (ii) $d(4, 19)$, (iii) $d(3, 99)$.
(b) Prove that the function d is a metric in X.
(c) Prove that the sequence $(2, 4, 8, \ldots, 2^n, \ldots)$ converges to 0.
(d) Prove that the sequence $(3, 6, 9, \ldots, 3n, \ldots)$ does not converge.
(e) Find a sequence of distinct elements of X such that the sequence converges to 5.
(f) Find the closure of the set $\{3, 6, 9, \ldots\}$. [Hint: First prove that, if n is any positive integer, then

$$k_n = \frac{2^{2n+1} + 1}{3}$$

is also a positive integer. For any $m \in X$ consider the sequence $(3k_1 m, 3k_2 m, 3k_3 m, \ldots)$ and show that this sequence converges to m.]

26. Review the definitions we have had for closed path, closed curve, closed surface, closed disk, closed ball, closed set. What similarities are there, and what differences?

8–3 Topological Spaces

In Section 8-2 we defined and discussed the concepts of open set, closed set, closure, and convergence in a metric space. The metric was used to define these concepts, and the properties of a metric (symmetry, triangle inequality, etc.) were used to derive certain properties of each of the new concepts. Any one of these concepts could be used to obtain a generalization of a metric space. This generalization would be obtained by starting with a set X, in which the appropriate concept is given axiomatically (not defined in terms of a more fundamental concept), and by studying the structure imposed on the set X by the axioms. We shall adopt "open set" as our fundamental concept and shall define other concepts in terms of this one.

A *topological space* is a set X, together with a family $\mathcal{O}$ of subsets of X satisfying the following conditions:

(O1) $X \in \mathcal{O}, \quad \emptyset \in \mathcal{O}$.

(O2) If $U \in \mathcal{O}$ and $V \in \mathcal{O}$, then $U \cap V \in \mathcal{O}$.

(O3) If $\mathcal{S} \subset \mathcal{O}$, then $\cup \{A : A \in \mathcal{S}\} \in \mathcal{O}$.

The members of the family $\mathcal{O}$ are called *open sets* in the topological space. This means that the statement "U is an open set" is equivalent to the statement "$U \in \mathcal{O}$."

Thus, in any topological space, the empty set and the set X itself are open sets; the intersection of any two open sets is open; and the union of any collection of open sets is open.

Before we give some examples of topological spaces, it is convenient to have another definition. A set $A \subset X$ is *closed* if and only if A' is open. Certainly the family $\mathcal{O}$ of all open sets in a topological space X completely determines the collection $\mathcal{C}$ of all closed sets. In fact,

$$\mathcal{C} = \{A : A' \in \mathcal{O}\}.$$

Conversely, the collection $\mathcal{C}$ also determines $\mathcal{O}$, since

$$\mathcal{O} = \{A : A' \in \mathcal{C}\}.$$

The three requirements O1 through O3 which were made above on the family $\mathcal{O}$ are easily seen to be equivalent to the conditions C1 through C3 below on the collection $\mathcal{C}$.

(C1) $\emptyset \in \mathcal{C}, \quad X \in \mathcal{C}$.

(C2) If $F \in \mathcal{C}$ and $G \in \mathcal{C}$, then $F \cup G \in \mathcal{C}$.

(C3) If $\mathcal{S} \subset \mathcal{C}$, then $\cap \{A : A \in \mathcal{S}\} \in \mathcal{C}$.

For a particular set X there may be several different families $\mathcal{O}$ of subsets of X which satisfy conditions O1 through O3, as shown by the examples below. The selection of one such family $\mathcal{O}$ is said to define a topology in the set X. Clearly, a topology in X may be defined by specifying a collection $\mathcal{C}$ of subsets of X which satisfies conditions C1 through C3, since the family $\mathcal{O}$ is then uniquely determined. This procedure is used in some of the following examples.

In each of Examples 3.1 through 3.5 the set X is the set of all real numbers; the topological spaces differ in the selection of the family $\mathcal{O}$ of open sets.

Example 3.1 $\mathcal{O}_1 = \{\emptyset, X\}$. From condition O1, this is the smallest family which defines a topology in X. In this topological space, $\mathcal{C}_1 = \{X, \emptyset\}$ so that a set is open iff it is closed.

Example 3.2 A subset $F \subset X$ is called *finite* iff F has a finite number of elements. For example: $\emptyset$ is finite, since it has 0 elements; the set $\{2, 3, 8\}$ is finite, since it has three elements; the set $N = \{1, 2, 3, \ldots\}$ is not finite. Let

$$\mathcal{F} = \{F : F \subset X \quad \text{and} \quad F \text{ is a finite set}\}$$

and let

$$\mathcal{C}_2 = \mathcal{F} \cup \{X\}.$$

Then $\mathcal{C}_2$ satisfies the conditions C1 through C3 and is, therefore, the collection of all closed sets in some topology defined in X. In this topological space, every finite set is closed, the set X is closed, and no other sets are closed. The family of open sets is given by

$$\mathcal{O}_2 = \{A : A = \emptyset \quad \text{or} \quad A' \text{ is a finite subset of } X\}.$$

Example 3.3 Let us call a set A *denumerable* iff there is a one-to-one transformation of A into the set $N = \{1, 2, 3, \ldots\}$ of all positive integers. Every finite set is denumerable, but there are also infinite denumerable sets; for example, the set $\{2, 4, 6, \ldots\}$ is denumerable, as is the set N itself. Problem 7 of Section 7-2 shows that the set of all positive rational numbers is denumerable, whereas the set $\{x : 0 \le x \le 1\}$ is not denumerable. Let

$$\mathcal{D} = \{A : A \subset X \quad \text{and} \quad A \text{ is denumerable}\},$$

and let $\mathcal{C}_3 = \mathcal{D} \cup \{X\}$. Then $\mathcal{C}_3$ is the collection of all closed sets in some topology defined in X. In this topological space, every denumerable set is closed; the set X is closed; and no other sets are closed. The family of open sets is given by

$$\mathcal{O}_3 = \{A : A = \emptyset \quad \text{or} \quad A' \text{ is a denumerable subset of } X\}.$$

Example 3.4 Set $\mathcal{O}_4 = \{A : A \subset X\}$. The family $\mathcal{O}_4$ satisfies conditions O1 through O3; it is evidently the largest family which defines a topology in X. (The topology defined by $\mathcal{O}_4$ is called the *discrete* topology.) In this topology it is again true that a set is open iff it is closed; i.e., $\mathcal{O}_4 = \mathcal{C}_4$. We have met this topological space before as a metric space. The family $\mathcal{O}_4$ is the collection of all sets which are open in the metric space X, where the distance between points x and y is given by

$$d(x, y) = \begin{cases} 0, & \text{if } x = y. \\ 1, & \text{if } x \neq y. \end{cases}$$

Example 3.5 For each real number $x \in X$, let

$$L_x = \{y : y < x\}$$

and let

$$\mathcal{L} = \{L_x : x \in X\}.$$

Then the set

$$\mathcal{O}_5 = \mathcal{L} \cup \{\emptyset, X\}$$

defines a topology in X.

PROBLEMS

1. Prove that each of Examples 3.1 through 3.5 is a topological space. What is the collection of closed sets in Example 3.5?

2. Show that if X is any metric space and $\mathcal{O}$ is the collection of all subsets of X which are open in that metric space, then $\mathcal{O}$ satisfies conditions O1 through O3, so X can be considered to be a topological space. Thus the two concepts of open set — one in a metric space and one in a topological space — need not cause any confusion.

3. Show that not every topological space can be thought of as a metric space. (Hint: Try the space of Example 3.1.)

4. Let X be the set of real numbers and let

$$I = \{x : 0 \leq x \leq 1\}.$$

Which of the following families defines a topology in X?
(a) $\mathcal{O} = \{A : I \subset A \subset X\} \cup \{\emptyset\}$.
(b) $\mathcal{O} = \{A : A \subset I\} \cup \{X\}$.
(c) $\mathcal{O} = \{A : I \not\subset A \text{ and } A \not\subset I\} \cup \{\emptyset, X\}$.

#5. Let X be the set of all continuous functions defined on the unit interval

$$I = \{t : 0 \leq t \leq 1\}$$

and let $\mathcal{O}$ be the family of all subsets U of X which satisfy the following condition: If $x_0 \in U$, then there are a positive number ε, a positive integer n, and n numbers $t_1 \in I, t_2 \in I, \ldots, t_n \in I$ such that

$$U \supset \{x: |x(t_i) - x_0(t_i)| < \varepsilon \ (i = 1, 2, \ldots, n)\}.$$

Prove that X, together with the family $\mathcal{O}$, is a topological space.

#6. Let $I^* = \{t: 0 \leq t\}$ and let X be the set of all continuous functions defined on I^*. Define a family $\mathcal{O}$ of subsets of X as in Problem 5 and prove that X, together with this family $\mathcal{O}$, is a topological space.

In our definition of a continuous transformation between metric spaces, the distance concept played a major role, since the definition was concerned with ε-nearness, etc. Of course, ε-nearness has no meaning in a general topological space, but the condition of Theorem 2.3, which is necessary and sufficient for continuity of a transformation between metric spaces, is meaningful in the general situation, and we use this condition to extend our definition of continuity.

Let X and Y be topological spaces; a transformation $f: X \rightarrow Y$ is *continuous* if and only if, for every open set $V \subset Y$, the set $f^{-1}(V)$ is open in X. Notice that this definition is concerned with continuity, and not with "continuity at x_0." It would be possible to extend this latter concept to transformations between topological spaces, but we shall not do so. A *homeomorphism* is a continuous transformation which has a continuous inverse transformation.

Example 3.6 Let each of X and Y be the topological space of Example 3.5; define two transformations $f: X \rightarrow Y$ and $g: X \rightarrow Y$ by setting

$$f(x) = \begin{cases} -1, & \text{if } x < 0. \\ x, & \text{if } x \geq 0. \end{cases} \qquad g(x) = \begin{cases} -1, & \text{if } x < 0. \\ 0, & \text{if } x = 0. \\ 1, & \text{if } x < 0. \end{cases}$$

Since X and Y are the same topological space, we could call them both X, but in the definition of continuity the two spaces are treated differently, so it is convenient to have a notation that indicates which space is being considered. We shall show that f is continuous, but g is not. First, consider f and let V be any open set in Y. We distinguish several cases, as follows:

CASE 1. $V = \emptyset$. Then $f^{-1}(V) = \emptyset$, which is open in X.

CASE 2. $V = Y$. Then $f^{-1}(V) = X$, which is open in X.

CASE 3. $V = L_y = \{z: z < y\}$.

(a) If $y \leq -1$, then $f^{-1}(V) = \emptyset$, which is open in X.

(b) If $-1 < y \leq 0$, then $f^{-1}(V) = \{x : x < 0\}$, which is open in X.

(c) If $0 < y$, then $f^{-1}(V) = \{x : x < y\}$, which is open in X.

Thus, for every open set $V \subset Y$, the set $f^{-1}(V)$ is open in X, and this proves that $f : X \to Y$ is continuous.

Now consider the transformation g. Set $V = \{y : y < \frac{1}{2}\}$; then V is an open subset of Y, but $f^{-1}(V) = \{x : x \leq 0\}$, which is not an open subset of X. Thus, $g : X \to Y$ is not continuous.

We define the concept of closure in a topological space X exactly as in a metric space. The *closure* A^- of a set $A \subset X$ is the smallest closed set having A as a subset.

It is easy to prove, from condition C3, that every set $A \subset X$ has a closure; that is, that there is a smallest closed set having A as a subset. Also, for any set A, its closure A^- is a closed set, and, in fact, A is closed iff $A = A^-$.

We have been concerned with the boundary, or edge, of a set on several occasions in our previous work, but we have not had a clear definition of this term. We can now define it. The *boundary* of a set A in a topological space X is the set $A^- \cap (A')^-$.

Thus, a point $x \in X$ is in the boundary of A iff

$$x \in A^- \quad \text{and} \quad x \in (A')^-.$$

We can think of the points of A^- as the points which are stuck very tightly onto A; from this viewpoint, the boundary of A is composed of all the points which are stuck very tightly onto A and also are stuck very tightly onto A'. This seems to be a quite satisfactory interpretation for the term boundary, or edge.

Notice that the boundary of a set A depends on the space X as well as on the particular set A. An example will clarify this point. Let X_1 be ordinary three-dimensional space; choose a particular point $x_0 \in X_1$ and consider the sphere $S = \{x : d(x_0, x) = 1\}$. This sphere is a closed set in the metric space X_1, and $(S')^- = X_1$. Thus the boundary of S is

$$S^- \cap (S')^- = S \cap X_1 = S.$$

The sphere is its own boundary when considered as a subset of ordinary three-dimensional space.

Now let X_2 be the sphere S, which is a metric space if we use the ordinary notion of distance, and again consider the subset S of X_2. The set S is closed, but $S' = \emptyset$, so, in the space X_2, the boundary of S is

$$S^- \cap (S')^- = S \cap \emptyset = \emptyset.$$

The boundary of the sphere is empty when the sphere is considered as a subset of itself.

In our previous work, when we mentioned the boundary of a piece of a surface, we have meant to think of this piece as a subset of the surface; when we have spoken of the boundary of a solid, we have meant to consider this solid as a subset of ordinary three-dimensional space.

PROBLEMS (continued)

7. Let each of X and Y be one of the topological spaces of Examples 3.1 through 3.5. Define a transformation $i: X \to Y$ by setting $i(x) = x$ for each $x \in X$. For which choices of X and Y is the transformation i continuous? For which choices is i a homeomorphism?

8. With X and Y as in Problem 7, define $f: X \to Y$ by setting $f(x) = x^2$. For which choices of X and Y is f continuous? For which choices is f a homeomorphism?

#9. (a) Let A be a subset of a topological space X and let x be a point of X. Prove that $x \in A^-$ iff every open set containing x contains at least one point of A.

(b) Prove that a transformation $f: X \to Y$ between two topological spaces is continuous iff, for every closed subset $F \subset Y$, $f^{-1}(F)$ is a closed subset of X.

10. For each of the following sets, consider it in turn as a subset of each of the topological spaces of Examples 3.1 through 3.5 and find the closure and the boundary of the set.

(a) $A = \{0, 1\}$.
(b) $B = \{x: 0 < x < 1\}$.
(c) $C = \{x: 0 < x \leq 1\}$.
(d) $D = \{x: 0 \leq x < 1\}$.
(e) $E = \{x: 0 \leq x \leq 1\}$.
(f) $F = \{x: x < 0\}$.
(g) $G = \{x: x \leq 0\}$.
(h) $H = \{x: x < 0 \quad \text{or} \quad x > 1\}$.
(i) $I = \{x: x \leq 0 \quad \text{or} \quad x \geq 1\}$.
(j) $J = \{x: x \leq 0 \quad \text{and} \quad x \geq 1\}$.

11. Review the places in our previous work where we have discussed the boundary of a set (*see* pp. 44, 63, 65, 78, 89).

12. Prove the following statements made in the text: If X is a topological space, then every subset A of X has a closure; A^- is a closed set; and, in fact, A is closed iff $A = A^-$.

13. Let X be a set and let $^-$ be a unary operation such that, for any $A \subset X$, A^- is also a subset of X. Suppose, further, that for any subsets A and B of X

$$\text{(a) } \emptyset^- = \emptyset. \qquad \text{(c) } A^{--} = A^-.$$

$$\text{(b) } A^- \supset A. \qquad \text{(d) } A^- \cup B^- = (A \cup B)^-.$$

Set $\mathcal{C} = \{A : A \subset X \text{ and } A^- = A\}$. Prove that $\mathcal{C}$ satisfies the conditions C1 through C3, so X may be thought of as a topological space. What is the closure operation in this space?

We now turn our attention to convergence of sequences in topological spaces. In a metric space, open balls were used to define convergence of sequences. How can we generalize this concept to topological spaces? An open ball $B(x; r)$ may be thought of as establishing a standard of nearness; it consists of all the points which are r-near to x. We have seen that an open set containing a point x can be thought of as containing all the points "right around" x. Thus we may think of each open set U containing x as setting up a standard of "nearness to x." Namely, all the points of U can be called U-near to x, and the points of U' can be said to be not U-near to x. The ideas involved in the convergence of (x_n) to x in a metric space can now be paraphrased as follows: A sequence (x_n) converges to x iff, given any open ball $B = B(x; \varepsilon)$ (a standard of nearness to x), the sequence (x_n) is eventually in B (eventually near to x, according to the given standard of nearness). These ideas generalize immediately to topological spaces and suggest the following definition.

A sequence (x_n) in a topological space X *converges* to the point $x \in X$ iff the sequence is eventually in each open set containing x.

Example 3.1 (continued) In the space X of Example 3.1, let (x_n) be any sequence and let x be any point. The only open set containing x is X itself, and certainly (x_n) is eventually in X. Thus, the sequence (x_n) converges to x. That is, in this topological space, any sequence converges to all points of X. In particular, limits of sequences in topological spaces may not be unique.

We have seen that, in a metric space, a point x is in the closure of a set A iff there is a sequence of points in A which converges to x. This pleasant state of affairs does not carry over to topological spaces (see Problem 16). There are some (non-metric) topological spaces for which the statement is true, and there are generalizations of the concept of sequence for which the analogous statement is true in any topological space, but we shall not go further into these matters here. Problem 9a above gives a characterization of the closure of a set which involves some of the ideas which we have used as the basis of convergence.

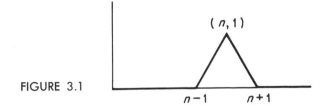

FIGURE 3.1

Example 3.7 Let X be the topological space of Problem 6 above; let $x_n \in X$ be the function whose graph is shown in Fig. 3.1; and let x_0 be the function defined by

$$x_0(t) = 0 \qquad (0 \le t).$$

We shall show that the sequence (x_n) converges to x_0. In fact, if U is any open set containing x_0, then there are a positive number ε, a positive integer m, and m non-negative numbers $t_1, t_2, \ldots, t_m$ such that

$$U \supset \{x: |x(t_i) - x_0(t_i)| < \varepsilon \qquad (i = 1, 2, \ldots, m)\}.$$

Let us set

$$n_0 = \max\{t_1, t_2, \ldots, t_m\}.$$

Then, clearly, if $n > n_0$, it follows that

$$x_n(t_i) = 0 \qquad (i = 1, 2, \ldots, m).$$

Hence

$$|x_n(t_i) - x_0(t_i)| = 0 < \varepsilon \qquad (i = 1, 2, \ldots, m)$$

and $x_n \in U$ for all $n > n_0$. That is, the sequence (x_n) is eventually in every open set which contains x_0; consequently, $x_n \to x_0$.

PROBLEMS (continued)

14. Which sequences converge to which points in the topological spaces of Examples 3.2 through 3.5?

15. Which sequences converge to which points in the topological spaces of Problem 4?

16. Give an example of a topological space X and a subset $A \subset X$ such that there is a point $x \in A^-$ and no sequence in A converges to x. (Hint: Try the space of Example 3.3.)

17. Show that, in Example 3.7, the function x_0 is the only function to which the sequence (x_n) converges.

18. Let X be the topological space of Problem 6. Define a sequence (x_n) in X by setting

$$x_n(t) = 2^{-(t-n)^2}.$$

Does this sequence converge? If so, to what function?

19. (a) Let X be the topological space of Problem 5 and let R be the metric space of real numbers with

$$d(r_1, r_2) = |r_1 - r_2|$$

for any real numbers r_1, r_2. For $x \in X$ and $t \in I = \{t : 0 < t < 1\}$,
$$x(t) \in R.$$

Thus, if (x_n) is a sequence in X and $t \in I$, then $(x_n(t))$ is a sequence in R. Prove that (x_n) converges to x_0 in the topological space X iff, for each $t \in I$; $(x_n(t))$ converges to $x_0(t)$ in the metric space R. This convergence of functions is called *pointwise convergence*.
(b) Prove that the result in part (a) remains valid if X is replaced by the topological space of Problem 6 and I is replaced by $I^* = \{t : t \geq 0\}$.

20. Generalize the results of Problem 19, Section 8-2 to topological spaces X to obtain the following results:
(a) If $p \in X$ and $x_n = p$, $n = 1, 2, \ldots$, then (x_n) converges to p.
(b) If $x_n \to x_0$ and $n_1 < n_2 < \cdots$, then $(x_{n_1}, x_{n_2}, \ldots)$ converges to x_0.
(c) Find an example of a sequence (x_n) in a topological space such that $x_n \to x$ and $x_n \to y$ but $x \neq y$. (This shows that the result of Problem 19d, Section 8-2 does not generalize to topological spaces. Problem 19c, Section 8-2 is considered in Problem 22 below.)

#21. Let X be a plane with its points labelled in rectangular coordinates; that is,

$$X = \{(x_1, x_2) : x_1 \text{ and } x_2 \text{ are real numbers}\}.$$

For each point $p = (p_1, p_2) \in X$, set

$$G_p = \{(x_1, x_2) : x_1 > p_1 \text{ and } x_2 > p_2\}.$$

Let $\mathcal{O}$ be the family of all unions of sets of the form G_p; that is, $U \in \mathcal{O}$ iff there is a subset $P \subset X$ with

$$U = \cup \{G_p : p \in P\}.$$

(a) Show that X, together with the family $\mathcal{O}$, is a topological space.

(b) Let $x_n = (-1/n, 1/n)$. Does the sequence (x_n) converge? If so, to what?

(c) Find the closure of the set $A = \{x_1, x_2, x_3, \ldots\}$ [notation of part (b)].

*22. Let X be the subset of a plane made up of the origin together with all the points whose coordinates are positive integers;

$$X = \{(0, 0)\} \cup \{(m, n): m = 1, 2, \ldots, n = 1, 2, \ldots\}.$$

However, the topology in X (defined below) is not the usual topology. For each positive integer m_0, the set

$$C_{m_0} = \{(m_0, n): n = 1, 2, \ldots\}$$

is called the *column at* m_0 in X. The open sets in X are defined as follows.

Any subset of X which does not contain the origin is open.

A subset U of X which does contain the origin is open iff there is a positive integer N such that if $m \geq N$ then U contains all but a finite number of the points in the column at m.

(a) Prove that X, with the open sets defined above, is a topological space.

(b) Find a sequence (x_n) in X such that (x_n) is frequently in each open set containing the origin but no subsequence of (x_n) converges to the origin. (This shows that the result of Problem 19c, Section 8-2 does not generalize to topological spaces.)

8–4 Connected Sets

We have defined the faces of a map to be the separate pieces into which a surface is divided by a network in that surface. But what is a piece? Evidently it is not the same as a subset, because two of the things we have thought of as faces would form a single subset of the surface, but not a single face of the map. We have several times used the phrase "connected pieces" but we have not had a definition of the term "connected." In discussing the Jordan curve theorem, we showed that certain pairs of points could be joined by a polygonal path; these ideas could be used to define a connected set in three-dimensional space, but a different approach is needed for an arbitrary topological space. It seems to be more convenient to define "separated" first, and then use this concept to define "connected." Intuitively, we would like to call two sets P and Q separated if, somehow, they have "nothing to do with each other." The exact formulation which has been found most fruitful is as follows: The subsets P and Q of a topological space X are *separated* iff

$$P \neq \emptyset \neq Q \quad \text{and} \quad P^- \cap Q = \emptyset = P \cap Q^-.$$

That is, neither set is empty, and each set is disjoint from the closure of the other. As an example, consider an X-axis (as a subset of three-dimensional space). Set

$$P = \{x: x < 0\}, \qquad Q = \{x: x > 0\}, \qquad S = \{x: x \geq 0\}.$$

Then P and Q are separated, but P and S are not separated.

A subset $A \subset X$ is *connected* iff A is not the union of two separated sets. In the X-axis just discussed, the set $\{x: x \neq 0\}$ is not connected because it is the union of the two separated sets P and Q.

In any topological space, a singleton (a set containing exactly one point) is connected. For, if

$$\{a\} = P \cup Q \quad \text{and} \quad P \neq \emptyset \neq Q,$$

then $P = \{a\} = Q$ so that

$$P^- \cap Q \neq \emptyset.$$

Thus, $\{a\}$ is not the union of two separated sets.

Example 4.1 In the topological space X of Example 3.1, every subset A is connected. For, if

$$A = P \cup Q \quad \text{and} \quad P \neq \emptyset \neq Q,$$

then $P^- = X$ (X is the only closed set containing P), and

$$P^- \cap Q \neq \emptyset.$$

Thus A is not the union of two separated sets.

Of course, whether or not a set A is connected depends on the topological space under consideration; the same set may be a connected subset of one space and not connected when it is considered as a subset of another space.

It seems plausible that, if a set A is connected, and if we adjoin to A the points which are "very close" to A, then the enlarged set is also connected. The following theorem makes this notion precise.

Theorem 4.1 If A is a connected subset of a topological space X, then A^- is connected.

PROOF. The proof is by contradiction. Suppose A^- is not connected; then $A^- = P \cup Q$, where P and Q are separated sets. If each of $A \cap P$ and $A \cap Q$ is non-empty, then

$$A = (A \cap P) \cup (A \cap Q)$$

expresses A as the union of two separated sets, contrary to our hypothesis. Thus, at least one of these sets is empty, say $A \cap P = \emptyset$. Then, since $A \subset P \cup Q$, it follows that $A \subset Q$. This implies that $A^- \subset Q^-$. But then

$$P \subset P \cup Q = A^- \subset Q^-$$

so that $P = P \cap Q^- = \emptyset$, which contradicts the assumption that P and Q are separated sets «.

Connectedness is a topological property of sets; in fact, the following theorem shows that if a set is connected it remains connected, even when it is subjected to a much more general class of transformations than the homeomorphisms.

Theorem 4.2 Let X and Y be topological spaces; let A be a connected subset of X, and let $f: X \to Y$ be a continuous transformation. Then $f(A)$ is a connected subset of Y.

PROOF. The proof is by contradiction. If $f(A)$ is not connected, then $f(A) = P \cup Q$ with P and Q separated. Set

$$P_1 = f^{-1}(P) \cap A, \quad \text{and} \quad Q_1 = f^{-1}(Q) \cap A;$$

then we find

$$P_1 \neq \emptyset \neq Q_1 \quad \text{and} \quad A = P_1 \cup Q_1.$$

Since f is continuous, $f^{-1}(P^-)$ is a closed set in X (Problem 9b, Section 8-3) which has P_1 as a subset; thus, $P_1^- \subset f^{-1}(P^-)$ and

$$P_1^- \cap Q_1 \subset f^{-1}(P^-) \cap f^{-1}(Q) = f^{-1}(P^- \cap Q) = f^{-1}(\emptyset) = \emptyset.$$

Similarly, $P_1 \cap Q_1^- = \emptyset$, so P_1 and Q_1 are separated. This contradicts the hypothesis that A is connected «.

The metric space R of the real numbers with

$$d(x, y) = |x - y|$$

for any two points x and y of R is a very important space. We have frequently used this space as an example, and many of the concepts in topology have arisen as generalizations of properties of the real numbers. In the remainder of the text, we shall denote this metric space by R and shall consider some of its properties. In the metric space R, the set R is connected. This fact is sometimes taken as one of the axioms used in defining the real numbers, and sometimes proved from other results which are taken as axioms. We shall assume this result and shall find what other subsets of R are connected.

A subset of R will be called an *interval* iff, for some points $a \in R$ and $b \in R$, it is one of the following sets:

$$\{x: a < x < b\} \qquad \{x: a \le x \le b\} \qquad \{x: x < b\}$$
$$\{x: a \le x < b\} \qquad \{x: a < x\} \qquad \{x: x \le b\}$$
$$\{x: a < x \le b\} \qquad \{x: a \le x\} \qquad R$$

Some examples of intervals are $\emptyset$, $\{2\}$, $\{x: 0 \le x < 1\}$. It is easy to see that a set $A \subset R$ is an interval if and only if it contains all points which lie between any two of its members; that is, iff the following implication is true. If

$$x \in A \quad \text{and} \quad y \in A \quad \text{and} \quad x < z < y,$$

then

$$z \in A.$$

We shall use this characterization of intervals in proving the following theorem.

Theorem 4.3 A subset $A \subset R$ is connected if and only if it is an interval.

PROOF. Suppose that $A \subset R$ and A is not an interval; then there are three real numbers $a < c < b$ such that

$$a \in A, \qquad b \in A, \qquad c \notin A.$$

Set

$$P = \{x: x \in A \quad \text{and} \quad x < c\}, \qquad Q = \{x: x \in A \quad \text{and} \quad x > c\}.$$

Then $P \ne \emptyset \ne Q$, and

$$P^- \cap Q \subset \{x: x \le c\} \cap Q = \emptyset.$$

Similarly, $P \cap Q^- = \emptyset$, so P and Q are separated. Thus A is not connected.

It remains to be proved that every interval is connected. First, let us consider the interval

$$I = \{x: 0 < x < 1\}.$$

For $x \in R$, set

$$f(x) = \frac{x}{|x| + 1},$$

then $f: R \rightarrow I$ is a transformation from R onto I. We prove below that f is continuous; since R is assumed to be connected, Theorem 4.2 shows that I is connected.

As to the continuity of f, if x and y have the same sign, then

$$|f(x) - f(y)| = \left| \frac{(|y| + 1)x - (|x| + 1)y}{(|x| + 1)(|y| + 1)} \right|$$

$$= \left| \frac{x - y}{(|x| + 1)(|y| + 1)} \right| \leq |x - y|.$$

If x and y do not have the same sign, then

$$|f(x) - f(y)| = \left| \frac{x}{|x| + 1} - \frac{y}{|y| + 1} \right| = \frac{|x|}{|x| + 1} + \frac{|y|}{|y| + 1}$$

$$\leq |x| + |y| = |x - y|$$

and continuity follows.

By Theorem 4.1, $I^- = \{x: 0 \leq x \leq 1\}$ is connected. The remainder of the proof of Theorem 4.3 is left as an exercise (Problem 5)«.

PROBLEMS

1. Prove that the empty set $\emptyset$ is connected.

2. (a) Prove that, in the space of Example 3.4, no set containing more than one point is connected.
   (b) Let Y be the space of Example 3.4 and let X be any topological space. Prove that X is connected iff every continuous transformation $f: X \rightarrow Y$ is constant.

3. Which sets are connected in the space of Example 3.5?

4. (a) Prove that if A and B are connected subsets of a topological space X and $A \cap B \neq \emptyset$, then $A \cup B$ is connected.
   (b) Prove that if A is connected and $A \subset B \subset A^-$, then B is connected.

5. The following steps complete the proof of Theorem 4.3.
   (a) Suppose $a \in R$, $b \in R$, and $a < b$. For

$$x \in I = \{x: 0 < x < 1\},$$

   define

$$f(x) = \tfrac{1}{2}[(b - a)x + (b + a)].$$

   Show that f is a continuous transformation from I onto $\{x: a < x < b\}$. Hence, this latter set is connected by Theorem 4.2.

(b) For each $a \in R$, define a continuous transformation f_a from R onto $L_a = \{x : x < a\}$, thus proving that L_a is connected.

(c) Complete the proof of Theorem 4.3 by considering each of the remaining types of intervals. (Hint: Use Problem 4 for some of the cases.)

6. Let $f : R \to R$ be a continuous transformation, and let a, b, and r be three real numbers such that

$$f(a) < r < f(b).$$

Prove that there is a $c \in R$ with $a < c < b$ and $f(c) = r$. Briefly stated: f takes on every value between any two of its values.

7. (a) Let A and B be two non-empty open subsets of a topological space X such that neither one is a subset of the other. Prove that $A - B$ and $B - A$ are separated.

(b) Replace "open" by "closed" in part (a) and prove the same result.

*8. For the topological space of Problem 21, Section 8-3, which of the following sets are connected?

(a) $A = \{(x_1, x_2) : x_1^2 + x_2^2 \leq 1\}$.
(b) $B = \{(x_1, x_2) : 2 \leq x_1^2 + x_2^2 \leq 4\}$.
(c) $C = A \cup B$.
(d) $D = A \cup \{(x_1, x_2) : (x_1 - 4)^2 + (x_2 - 4)^2 < 1\}$.
(e) $E = A \cup \{(x_1, x_2) : (x_1 - 4)^2 + (x_2 + 4)^2 < 1\}$.

9. Review the places in our previous work where we have required a set to be "all in one piece" (*see* pp. 60, 63, 74ff, 78, 89).

8–5 Compact Sets

A family $\mathcal{F} = \{F : F \in \mathcal{F}\}$ of subsets of a topological space X is called a *cover* of a set $A \subset X$ iff

$$A \subset \cup \{F : F \in \mathcal{F}\}.$$

A cover is an *open cover* iff each set in the family is an open set. A *subcover* of a cover $\mathcal{F}$ is a subfamily of the family $\mathcal{F}$ which is also a cover (of the same set A). For example, if A is a subset of a metric space X, the collection $\mathcal{B}$ of all open balls in X is an open cover of A; the collection of all open balls with center in A and radius 1 is a subcover of $\mathcal{B}$.

We use this terminology in defining compactness. A set A in a topological space X is *compact* iff every open cover of A has a finite subcover. Evidently, in any topological space X, any finite set

$$A = \{a_1, a_2, \ldots, a_n\} \subset X$$

is compact. For, if $\mathcal{U} = \{U : U \in \mathcal{U}\}$ is an open cover of A, and $1 \leq i \leq n$, we may choose an element $U_i \in \mathcal{U}$ such that $a_i \in U_i$. The family $U_1, U_2, \ldots, U_n$ is a finite subcover of $\mathcal{U}$.

The metric space R is not compact, because if we set

$$I_n = \{x : n - \tfrac{1}{4} < x < n + \tfrac{5}{4}\}$$

then

$$\mathcal{U} = \{I_n : n = \ldots, -1, 0, 1, \ldots\}$$

is an open cover of R, which has no finite subcover. Before considering other examples, we shall discuss certain consequences of compactness.

A family $\mathcal{F}$ of sets is said to have the *finite intersection property* iff every finite subfamily of $\mathcal{F}$ has a non-empty intersection. Theorem 5.1 characterizes compact spaces, using the finite intersection property.

Theorem 5.1 A topological space X is compact iff, whenever $\mathcal{F}$ is a family of closed sets with the finite intersection property, the intersection $\cap \{F : F \in \mathcal{F}\}$ of all the sets in $\mathcal{F}$ is not empty.

PROOF. Suppose X is not compact; then there is an open cover $\mathcal{U}$ of X which has no finite subcover. Set $\mathcal{F} = \{F : F' \in \mathcal{U}\}$; $\mathcal{F}$ is a family of closed sets. If $\{F_1, F_2, \ldots, F_n\}$ is any finite subfamily of $\mathcal{F}$, the collection

$$\mathcal{U}_1 = \{F_1', F_2', \ldots, F_n'\}$$

is a finite subfamily of $\mathcal{U}$. Since $\mathcal{U}_1$ is not a cover of X, there is a point $x \in X$ such that

$$x \notin F_i' \qquad (i = 1, 2, \ldots, n).$$

Clearly,

$$x \in F_1 \cap F_2 \cap \ldots \cap F_n,$$

and $\mathcal{F}$ has the finite intersection property. Since $\mathcal{U}$ is a cover of X, each point $x \in X$ is contained in some $U \in \mathcal{U}$, and, consequently, $x \notin U' \in \mathcal{F}$. Thus no point of X is contained in all the sets $F \in \mathcal{F}$;

$$\cap \{F : F \in \mathcal{F}\} = \emptyset.$$

Now suppose X is compact, and let $\mathcal{F}$ be a family of closed sets such that

$$\cap \{F : F \in \mathcal{F}\} = \emptyset.$$

Then

$$\mathcal{U} = \{U : U' \in \mathcal{F}\}$$

is an open cover of X and, since X is compact, there is a finite subcover $\{U_1, U_2, \ldots, U_n\}$. Set

$$F_i = U_i' \qquad (i = 1, 2, \ldots, n);$$

then

$$(\cap F_i)' = \cup (F_i') = \cup (U_i) = X.$$

Thus, $\underset{i}{\cap} F_i = \emptyset$ and $\mathcal{F}$ does not have the finite intersection property «.

The statement of Theorem 5.1 is useful in proving certain existence theorems. Suppose X is compact and that we want to prove the existence of a point $x \in X$ which satisfies an infinite number of given conditions. That is, we want to prove that the conditions are consistent. If, for each one of the conditions, the set of points satisfying that condition is closed, and if each finite collection of the conditions is consistent, then Theorem 5.1 asserts that there is a point which satisfies all the conditions.

In a compact subset of a metric space, convergence of sequences is somewhat well behaved, as the following theorem shows.

Theorem 5.2 If A is a compact subset of a metric space X and (x_n) is a sequence in A, then some subsequence of (x_n) converges to a point of A.

PROOF. By Problem 19c, Section 8-2, it is sufficient to show that there is a point $x_0 \in A$ such that (x_n) is frequently in each open set containing x_0. The proof is by contradiction. Suppose that no such point x_0 exists; then for each point $x \in A$ there is an open set U_x containing x such that U_x contains only a finite number of the points in the sequence (x_n). The family

$$\mathcal{U} = \{U_x : x \in A\}$$

is an open cover of the compact set A, so there is a finite subcover, say $\{U_1, U_2, \ldots, U_m\}$. Since each set in this finite subcover contains only a finite number of terms of the sequence (x_n), there is only a finite number of the terms of this sequence in the union

$$U_1 \cup U_2 \cup \cdots \cup U_m.$$

But this is absurd, because (x_n) is in A, and A is a subset of this union «.

Theorem 5.2 gives the intuitive meaning of the term "compact." The term should mean that the points of the set are somehow "jammed closely together," and Theorem 5.2 asserts that every sequence has a convergent subsequence; that is, a subsequence whose terms get "close" to something and, consequently, get close to each other. Theorem 5.2 is stated as an implication and not as an equivalence. It is also true that if A is a subset of a metric space such that every sequence in A has a subsequence which converges to a point of A, then A is compact. [For a proof, *see* (Ref. 19, Theorem 4.16, *p.* 109)].

The concept of compactness is a topological one; in fact, just as with connectedness, compactness survives under even more general transformations than homeomorphisms.

Theorem 5.3 Let X and Y be topological spaces; let $f: X \to Y$ be a continuous transformation and let A be a compact subset of X; then $f(A)$ is a compact subset of Y.

PROOF. If $\mathcal{V} = \{V: V \in \mathcal{V}\}$ is any open cover of $f(A)$, then

$$\mathcal{U} = \{f^{-1}(V): V \in \mathcal{V}\}$$

is an open cover of A. Since A is compact, there is a finite subcover

$$\{f^{-1}(V_i): i = 1, 2, \ldots, n\}$$

of $\mathcal{U}$. It follows that

$$\{V_i: i = 1, 2, \ldots, n\}$$

covers $f(A)$ and is a finite subcover of $\mathcal{V}$ «.

We have seen that the metric space R is not compact; however, there are some important compact subsets of R.

Theorem 5.4 In the space R, the set

$$I = \{x: 0 \le x \le 1\}$$

is compact.

PROOF. Let $\mathcal{U} = \{U: U \in \mathcal{U}\}$ be an open cover of I; we shall show that $\mathcal{U}$ has a finite subcover. The idea is that we shall start at 0 and see how far we can advance toward 1 by using a finite number of sets in $\mathcal{U}$. If we can reach 1, we shall have achieved our goal. For each $b \in I$, set

$$I_b = \{x: 0 \le x \le b\}$$

and define

$$B = \{b: b \in I \text{ and a finite number of sets in } \mathcal{U} \text{ cover } I_b\}.$$

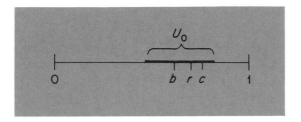

FIGURE 5.1

Evidently, $0 \in B$; no negative number is in B (since none is in I); and, if $c \in B$ and $0 < b < c$, then $b \in B$. Thus B is an interval. Let the real number r be the right-hand end point of B (there must be a right-hand end point, since $B \subset I$); we shall show that $r = 1$. If not, let U_0 be a member of $\mathfrak{U}$ such that $r \in U_0$ (Fig. 5.1). Choose two points b and c in U_0 with $b < r < c$. Then $b \in B$ so there is a finite subfamily

$$\{U_1, U_2, \ldots, U_n\}$$

of $\mathfrak{U}$ which covers I_b. But then

$$\{U_1, U_2, \ldots, U_n, U_0\}$$

covers I_c, which contradicts the definition of r as the right-hand end point of B. Thus $r = 1$.

We have proved so far that B is an interval with end points 0 and 1 and $0 \in B$. This leaves two possibilities: either

$$B_1 = \{x : 0 \le x \le 1\} \quad \text{or} \quad B_2 = \{x : 0 \le x < 1\}.$$

It can be seen, as above, that B cannot be B_2 since if $\mathfrak{U}$ has a finite subcover for I_b whenever $b \in B_2$, then, by adjoining one more set of $\mathfrak{U}$, we could obtain a finite cover of I itself. Thus $B = B_1$, and the theorem is proved **«**.

The compact subsets of R are further discussed in Problem 5.

Let X and Y be metric spaces with X compact. In this case, a continuous transformation $f: X \to Y$ satisfies a condition which is, in general, somewhat stronger than continuity. Recall that f is continuous iff, for every $\varepsilon > 0$ and every $x_0 \in X$, there is a $\delta > 0$ such that if x is δ-near to x_0 then $f(x)$ is ε-near to $f(x_0)$. We have seen (Example 3.5 in Chapter 7) that, in general, δ may depend on both x_0 and ε. If X is compact, δ can be chosen to depend on ε alone, and the same value of δ will satisfy the condition for all points $x_0 \in X$. We shall prove this theorem only in the special case where

$$X = I = \{x : 0 \le x \le 1\}.$$

Theorem 5.5 Let Y be a metric space and let $f: I \to Y$ be a continuous transformation. For any $\varepsilon > 0$ there is a $\delta > 0$ such that if a and b are points of I and $|a - b| < \delta$, then $f(a)$ and $f(b)$ are ε-near to each other.

Proof. Let $\varepsilon > 0$ be given. Since f is continuous, we may find, for each $x \in I$, an open ball $B_x = B(x; r_x)$ such that every point of $f(B_x)$ is $\frac{\varepsilon}{2}$-near to $f(x)$. The family

$$\mathcal{B} = \{B_x : x \in I\}$$

is an open cover of the compact set I; choose a finite subcover

$$\mathcal{B}_1 = \{B_{x_i} : i = 1, 2, \ldots, n\}.$$

Now (Problem 6) choose $\delta > 0$ so that if a and b are points of I and $|a - b| < \delta$, then there is one of the sets

$$B_{x_i} \qquad (i = 1, 2, \ldots, n)$$

which contains both a and b. If a and b are any points of I and $|a - b| < \delta$, choose x' so that a and b are both in $B_{x'}$ and denote the distance function in Y by e. We find that

$$e(f(a), f(b)) \leq e(f(a), f(x')) + e(f(x'), f(b)) \leq \frac{\varepsilon}{2} + \frac{\varepsilon}{2} = \varepsilon,$$

which is the required conclusion **«**.

PROBLEMS

1. (a) Prove that, in the space of Example 3.1, every subset is compact.
   (b) Prove that, in the space of Example 3.2, every subset is compact.
   (c) Which subsets of the space of Example 3.4 are compact?

2. Let X be a topological space and let A be a subset of X. Prove that A is compact iff, whenever $\mathcal{F}$ is a family of closed sets such that every finite intersection of sets of $\mathcal{F}$ meets A, then the intersection of all the sets of $\mathcal{F}$ meets A.

3. (a) Prove that, in a metric space, every compact set is closed.
   (b) Give an example of a compact subset A of a topological space such that A is not closed.

4. Prove that a closed subset of a compact set is compact.

5. (a) Prove that every compact subset of the metric space R is closed and bounded.

(**b**) Let a and b be any points in R; prove that $\{x: a \leq x \leq b\}$ is compact.

(**c**) Prove that a subset A of R is compact if and only if A is closed and bounded.

6. Let $I = \{x: 0 \leq x \leq 1\}$ be a subset of the metric space R and let

$$\mathcal{B}_1 = \{B(x_i; r_i): i = 1, 2, \ldots, n\}$$

be a cover of I composed of a finite number of open balls. Show that there is a $\delta > 0$ such that if a and b are points of I and $|a - b| < \delta$, then there is one of the open balls

$$B(x_i; r_i) \qquad (i = 1, 2, \ldots, n)$$

which contains both a and b.

7. Check the result of Theorem 5.5 in the case where $Y = R$ and $f: I \to Y$ is defined by

$$f(x) = (4x - 1)^2.$$

Given $\varepsilon > 0$, find a value of $\delta > 0$ such that the condition of the theorem is satisfied.

8–6 Complete Sets

The concept of completeness (defined below) is applicable in metric spaces, but not in all topological spaces; therefore, all the spaces discussed in this section will be metric spaces. A special property of sequences will be needed to define completeness.

A sequence (x_n) in a metric space X is a *Cauchy sequence* iff, given any $\varepsilon > 0$, there is a positive integer n_0 such that every two points in the sequence beyond the n_0th are ε-near to each other. Using d for the distance function in X, we can state the requirement after "such that" in this definition as follows: If $n > n_0$ and $m > n_0$, then $d(x_n, x_m) < \varepsilon$. The idea of the definition is that, if $\varepsilon > 0$, then eventually the points of the sequence are ε-near to each other. A metric space X is *complete* iff every Cauchy sequence in X converges to a point of X. A subset $A \subset X$ is *complete* iff every Cauchy sequence in A converges to a point of A.

Example 6.1 Let $X = \{x: x > 0\}$ be the set of all positive real numbers, and define

$$d(x, y) = |x - y|.$$

Set $x_n = 1/n$; then (x_n) is a Cauchy sequence, but there is no point of X to which this sequence converges. Thus X is not complete.

Example 6.2 Let X be any set and, for $x \in X$, $y \in X$, define

$$d(x, y) = \begin{cases} 0, & \text{if } x = y. \\ 1, & \text{if } x \neq y. \end{cases}$$

Then X is a metric space. If (x_n) is a Cauchy sequence in X, then, eventually, every pair of points of the sequence must be $\frac{1}{2}$-near to each other; but two points in X are $\frac{1}{2}$-near iff they are the same point. Thus, every Cauchy sequence in X must eventually be in a singleton. Evidently such a sequence does converge; the space X is complete.

Intuitively, something is complete if there is "nothing missing that should be there." The definition of a complete space requires that, for every sequence whose points are suitably near to each other, there must be a point in the space to which the sequence converges. This is a quite reasonable interpretation of "no points are missing that should be there."

Example 6.1 shows that a Cauchy sequence may not converge; the following theorem states that a convergent sequence must be a Cauchy sequence.

Theorem 6.1 If the sequence (x_n) converges to x in the metric space X, then (x_n) is a Cauchy sequence.

PROOF. Let $\varepsilon > 0$ be given. Since $x_n \to x$, the sequence is eventually in the open ball $B = B\left(x; \frac{\varepsilon}{2}\right)$. The proof is completed by noting that any two points of B are ε-near to each other ◀◀.

Theorem 6.2 A compact subset of a metric space is complete.

PROOF. Suppose A is a compact subset of the metric space X, and let (x_n) be a Cauchy sequence in A. By Theorem 5.2, some subsequence of (x_n) converges to a point of A, and this implies (Problem 4) that (x_n) converges to the same point ◀◀.

Example 6.3 The metric space R is complete, but not compact. We have seen in Section 8-5 that R is not compact; it remains to prove that R is complete. Let (x_n) be a Cauchy sequence in R and take $\varepsilon = 1$. From the Cauchy condition, there is a positive integer n_0 such that, for $n > n_0$, x_n is 1-near to x_{n_0}. Set

$$I = \{x : x_{n_0} - 1 \leq x \leq x_{n_0} + 1\};$$

then I is a compact subset of R (Problem 5c, Section 8-5), and I is complete by Theorem 6.2. The Cauchy sequence

$$(x_{n_0}, x_{n_0+1}, \ldots)$$

is in I; thus some subsequence of this sequence converges to a point of I, and the result follows.

We have seen that both connectedness and compactness are preserved under continuous transformations. This is not true of completeness. In fact, completeness is not even a topological concept, as the following example shows.

Example 6.4 Let R be the metric space of the real numbers and let

$$I = \{x: -1 < x < 1\},$$

with the distance in I defined by

$$d(x, y) = |x - y|.$$

Then R is complete (Example 6.3); but I is not complete, since the sequence $(1 - 1/n)$ is a Cauchy sequence in I, which does not converge to a point of I. But the transformation $f: R \to I$ defined by

$$f(x) = \frac{x}{|x| + 1}$$

is a homeomorphism (Problem 5). Thus R and I are topologically equivalent spaces; one of them is complete and the other is not; it follows that completeness is not a topological property.

There are many important theorems concerning complete spaces. The completeness of R asserts the existence of a real number which is the limit of the sequence

$$(1.4, 1.41, 1.412, \ldots).$$

If we define the nth term of this sequence to be the largest rational number, with denominator 10^n, whose square is less than 2, then it is quite easy to prove that the number which is the limit of this sequence must have its square equal to 2. Moreover, $\sqrt{2}$ is not a rational number; thus, the completeness of R implies the existence of irrational numbers. In fact, one of the standard procedures for constructing the real numbers from the rational numbers is by means of a process called completion by Cauchy sequences, but we shall not discuss this process here.

PROBLEMS

1. In the metric space R, which of the following sequences (x_n) are Cauchy sequences? For each of these Cauchy sequences, find the point to which it converges.

(a) $x_n = 1/n$.

(b) $x_n = (-1)^n(1/n)$.

(c) $x_n = 1 + (-1)^n(1/n)$.

(d) $x_n = (-1)^n(1 - 1/n)$.

(e) $x_n = n$.

(f) $x^n = n^{10}/n!$.

(g) $x_n = n/(n+1)$.

(h) $x_n = n^2/(n+1)$.

(i) $x_n = n/(n^2+1)$.

(j) $x_n = \sin n$.

2. Which of the following subsets of R are complete?

(a) The set of all rational numbers.

(b) The set of all irrational numbers.

(c) $I = \{x : 0 \le x \le 1\}$.

(d) $N = \{1, 2, 3, \ldots\}$.

(e) $T = \{2\}$.

(f) The empty set $\emptyset$.

3. (a) Prove that every closed subset of a complete space is complete.

(b) Prove that every complete subset of a metric space is closed.

4. Prove that if (x_n) is a Cauchy sequence in a metric space X and if some subsequence of (x_n) converges to a point $x \in X$, then the sequence (x_n) converges to x.

5. Prove that the transformation $f : R \to I$ in Example 6.4 is a homeomorphism.

6. Define x_n to be the largest rational number, with denominator 10^n, whose square is less than 2.

(a) Prove that (x_n) is a Cauchy sequence.

(b) Prove that the equation $x^2 = 2$ is satisfied by the real number x to which the Cauchy sequence (x_n) converges.

References

Chapter 0: 2, 3, 7, 9, 13, 14, 21, 25, 39.

Chapter 1: 16, 17.

Chapter 2: 5, 6, 11, 12, 15, 16, 18, 23, 24, 28, 30, 32, 35, 37, 38.

Chapter 3: 1, 6, 8, 11, 16, 18, 22, 23, 24, 30, 34.

Chapter 4: 5, 11, 16, 18, 22, 24, 30, 34.

Chapter 5: 6, 11, 24, 26, 27, 38.

Chapter 6: 9, 10, 20, 32.

Chapter 7: 4, 6, 11, 17, 19, 29, 31, 33, 34, 36.

Chapter 8: 6, 19, 29, 31, 34.

1. Aleksandrov, P. S., *Combinatorial Topology*, vol. **1,** trans. Horace Komm. Rochester: Graylock Press, 1956.

2. Allendoerfer, C. B., "Deductive Methods in Mathematics," *Insights into Modern Mathematics*, The National Council of Teachers of Mathematics, Twenty-third yearbook. Washington, D. C.: The National Council of Teachers of Mathematics, Inc., 1955.

3. —— and C. O. Oakley, *Principles of Mathematics*, chap. 1. New York: McGraw-Hill Book Company, Inc., 1955.

4. Artin, E., "On the Theory of Complex Functions," *Notre Dame Mathematical Lectures*, No. 4, pp. 55–70. Ann Arbor: University of Notre Dame, 1944.

5. Ball, W. W. R., *Mathematical Recreations and Essays*, rev. by H. S. M. Coxeter. New York: The Macmillan Company, 1947.

6. Bing, R. H., *"Elementary Point Set Topology,"* Herbert Ellsworth Slaught Memorial Paper No. 8, *American Mathematical Monthly*, vol. **57,** No. 7, Part II (1960).

7. Brumfiel, C. F., R. E. Eicholz, and M. E. Shanks, *Geometry*, chap. 2. Reading, Massachusetts: Addison-Wesley Publishing Company, Inc., 1960.

8. Cairns, S. S., *Introductory Topology*. New York: The Ronald Press Company, 1961.

9. Christian, R. R., *Introduction to Logic and Sets*. New York: Ginn and Company, 1958.

10. Committee on the Undergraduate Program, R. L. Davis, ed., *Elementary Mathematics of Sets with Applications*. Ann Arbor: Mathematical Association of America, 1958.

11. Courant, R. and H. Robbins, *What is Mathematics?* New York: Oxford University Press, 1941.

12. Errera, Alfred, "Une Vue d'Ensemble sur le Probleme des Quatre Couleurs," *Rendiconti del Seminario Matematico*, Università e Politecnico de Torino, vol. **11,** (1952), pp. 5–19.

13. Eves, Howard and C. V. Newsom, *An Introduction to the Foundations and Fundamental Concepts of Mathematics*. New York: Rinehart and Company, Inc., 1958.

14. Exner, R. M. and M. K. Rosskopf, *Logic in Elementary Mathematics*. New York: McGraw-Hill Company, Inc., 1959.

15. Franklin, Philip, "The Four Color Problem," *Scripta Mathematica*, vol. **6**, (1934), pp. 149–56, 197–210.

16. Frechet, M. and Ky Fan, *Introduction a la Topologie Combinatoire*. Paris: Vuibert, 1946.

17. Frenchel, W. F., "Elementare Beweise und Anwendungen einiger Fixpunktsätze," *Matematisk Tidsskrift*, **B** (1932), pp. 66–87.

18. Gardner, Martin, *The Scientific American Book of Mathematical Puzzles and Diversions*. New York: Simon and Schuster, 1959.

19. Hall, Dick Wick and G. L. Spencer, *Elementary Topology*. New York: John Wiley and Sons, Inc., 1955.

20. Halmos, P. R., *Naive Set Theory*. Princeton: D. VanNostrand Company, Inc., 1960.

21. Hempel, C. G., "On the Nature of Mathematical Proof," *American Mathematical Monthly*, vol. **52** (1945), pp. 543–56.

22. Hilbert, David and S. Cohn-Vossen, *Geometry and the Imagination*, trans. P. Nemenyi. New York: Chelsea Publishing Company, 1952.

23. Jones, B. M., *Elementary Concepts of Mathematics*. New York: The Macmillan Company, 1947.

24. Kasner, E. and J. Newman, *Mathematics and the Imagination*. New York: Simon and Schuster. 1940.

25. Kemeny, J. G., J. L. Snell, and G. L. Thompson, *Introduction to Finite Mathematics*. Englewood Cliffs, New Jersey: Prentice-Hall, Inc., 1957.

26. Kerékjártó, B., "Demonstration élémentaire du Théorème de Jordan sur les Courbes Planes," *Acta Scientiarum Mathematicarum*, Szeged, vol. **5** (1930), pp. 56–59.

27. Kline, J. R., "What is the Jordan Curve Theorem?" *American Mathematical Monthly*, vol. **49** (1942), pp. 281–86.

28. Kuratowski, C., "Sur le Problème des Courbes Gauches en Topologie," *Fundamentae Mathematicae*, vol. **15** (1930), pp. 271–83.

29. Lefschetz, S., *Introduction to Topology*. Princeton: Princeton University Press, 1949.

30. Lietzmann, Walther, *Anschauliche Topologie*. Munich: R. Oldenbourg, 1955.

31. Newman, M. H. A., *Elements of the Topology of Plane Sets of Points*, 2nd ed. Cambridge: Cambridge University Press, 1954.

32. Rademacher, H. and O. Toeplitz, *The Enjoyment of Mathematics*. Princeton: Princeton University Press, 1957.

33. Rado, T., "Length and Area," pp. 142–53. *American Mathematical Society Colloquium Publications*, vol. **30,** New York: American Mathematical Society, 1948.

34. Seifert, H. and W. Threlfall, *Lehrbuch der Topologie*. Leipzig: B. G. Teubner, 1934.

35. Steinhaus, H., *Mathematical Snapshots*. New York: Oxford University Press, 1950.

36. Tucker, A. W., "Some Topological Properties of Disk and Sphere," *Proceedings of the First Canadian Mathematical Congress*. Toronto: The University of Toronto Press, 1946, pp. 285–309.

37. —— and H. S. Bailey, Jr., "Topology," *Scientific American*, vol. **182** (1950), pp. 18–24.

38. Whyburn, G. T., "What is a Curve?" *American Mathematical Monthly*, vol. **49** (1942), pp. 493–97.

39. Wilder, R. L., "The Nature of Mathematical Proof," *American Mathematical Monthly*, vol. **51** (1944), pp. 301–23.

Index

arc 30

ball 59, 140
boundary 63, 156
Brouwer's theorem 132

cardinal number 114
Cauchy sequence 172
circle 58
closed 142
  ball 59, 140
  curve 58, 127
  disk 58
  path 32
  set 142, 152
  surface 65
closure 145, 156
compact 166
complement 106
complete 172
connected map 44
  network 31
  set 162
  simply 74
continuous transformation 119, 140, 155
converge 147, 158
  pointwise 160
counter example 7
cover 166
cut 75

denumerable 153
difference 106
direct proof 10
disjoint 105
disk 58
distance 138

edge of a map 44
elastic motion 23, 111, 123
empty set 100
ε-near 120, 140
equivalent statements 5
  topologically 24, 57ff, 123, 155
Euler's theorem 45, 77
even vertex 32
eventually 147

face 44
finite 153
  intersection property 167
fixed point 127
  property 132
  theorem 132

four color problem 43ff
frequently 147
fundamental theorem of algebra 133

Hamiltonian path 38
homeomorphism 122, 140, 155

identity transformation 113
implication 4
included 99
index of a transformation 127
indirect proof 11
induction hypothesis 15
  mathematical 13
initial vertex 32
intersection 105
interval 164
into 112
inverse image 113
  transformation 114

Jordan curve theorem 89

Klein bottle 67
Königsberg bridges 29

manifold 63
map 43
  connected 44
  regular 45
mathematical induction 13
meet 105
metric space 138
Möbius strip 66

181